An Introduction
to
Biblical Truths

An Introduction to Biblical Truths

REVISED EDITION

Alexander C. De Jong

BAKER BOOK HOUSE
Grand Rapids, Michigan

ISBN: 0-8010-2887-6
Revised Edition

PHOTOLITHOPRINTED BY CUSHING - MALLOY, INC.
ANN ARBOR, MICHIGAN, UNITED STATES OF AMERICA
1978

Foreword

Having frequently used the first edition of *What I Confess* in the instruction of people of various religious backgrounds, I welcome this revised edition. I found the former edition to be very helpful in the preparation of people for church membership.

Dr. Alexander De Jong has provided a substantial book of instruction within a rather limited number of pages. God's plan of salvation is clearly presented, as is the need for human response both in faith and life. The student using the book is introduced to the truth of Scripture as outlined in the Reformed Confessions. Teachers, of individuals or groups, will find the chapters to be broad summaries of truth, yet at any point one may easily dig deeper into areas that may be of particular interest or difficulty to the student.

The Appendix includes valuable material. The definitions of Christian terms in "A Basic Christian Vocabulary" will provide a handy reference for the person learning Christian terminology. The summaries of lessons found in Appendix I "What I Confess" are personal and succinct. New Christians will find these statements helpful in checking out their own understanding.

This book can surely be used by the Holy Spirit in the discipling of new Christians.

John G. Van Ryn
Executive Secretary
Christian Reformed Home Missions
Reformed Church in America

Preface

In this revised edition the Biblical text of the Revised Standard Version has been used instead of the American Standard Version. After each main section in the text there are completion sentences which summarize main ideas and can be used as discussion starters. Appendix I contains brief, personal confessions under "What I Confess," and "Digging Deeper" questions which enrich and expand the basic doctrines studied in the eight lessons. Added to the Appendix at the request of ministers and teachers who had used edition one are the "Review Questions and Answers." Appendix II contains a basic Christian vocabulary.

The format of this manual has been chosen to meet the needs of students of doctrine on various levels. The eight lessons present the basic teachings in a brief, concise manner, documented by Biblical references. The Appendixes provide enrichment material for those whose understanding has become more developed.

I am grateful to Mrs. Wilhelmina Zwiers, church secretary, who typed the revised manuscript, and to my wife Joanne who suggested revisions. I appreciate the interest of those who used the first edition with profit and encouraged me to prepare the new edition. But primarily I am thankful to our enabling Savior who is pleased to use the humblest of our efforts. May He use this manual for the building of His church, our spiritual mother.

Alexander C. De Jong
Oak Lawn, Ill.
August, 1977

Contents

LESSON 1

Getting To Know God

God refuses to debate the question, "Does God exist?" He does not permit the sinful luxury of treating His existence as a problem in geometry or as a laboratory specimen to be dissected. In the Bible God graciously condescends in many ways to tell us *who* He is. But He never stoops to argue *that* He is. The opening words of the Bible are, "In the beginning God created . . ." (Gen. 1:1). At the very close of Scripture God says, ". . . if any one takes away from the words of the book of this prophecy, God will take away his share in the tree of life" (Rev. 22:19). In laying down the moral law God says, "I am the Lord your God. . . . you shall have no other gods before me" (Exod. 20:2, 3). Without apology, with His divinely unique intolerance, God confronts man saying, "Thus says the Lord, the King of Israel, and his Redeemer, the Lord of hosts: I am the first and I am the last; besides me there is no god" (Isa. 44:6). God declares Himself.

Every man believes in a god of some kind. Because man is a human being made in God's image, he cannot help believing. He worships and devotes himself to something—some power, some person, some element in life. His god may be human reason, social success, community opinion, material goods, money, country, or—and this most often—himself. Therefore God does not argue His existence but rather calls man to acknowledge Him as He is and as He has made Himself known. The alternative of life is belief in a man-made god or belief in the self-revealing God. The issue today is as it was on Mount Carmel, "How long will you go limping with two opinions? If the Lord is God, follow him, but if Baal, then follow him" (I Kings 18:21).

1. God never stoops to argue that He ___________, but rather He ___________ Himself in many ways.
2. Every man believes in a ___________ of some kind.

God Is a Triune God

God is the one God who lives as Father, Son, and Holy Spirit. The Westminster Shorter Cathechism describes the doctrine of the Trinity in these words: "There are three persons within the Godhead; the Father, the Son, and the Holy Ghost (Spirit); and these three are one God, the same in substance, equal in power and glory."

To some this statement can be a baffling question of arithmetic, a puzzling juggling of numbers. However, the Christian does not claim to teach that God is one and three in the same sense. The doctrine is indeed a mystery, but it is not a numerical contradiction.

The doctrine of the Trinity means that God is one in one respect, namely in substance or essence. "Hear, O Israel: the Lord our God is one Lord . . ." (Deut. 6:4). Yet the Bible is equally clear in asserting that the one God exists as three distinct persons, as Father, Son, and Holy Spirit. The threeness of God's Trinitarian life concerns these personal distinctions. When the church confesses that the living God is a triune God, it states that the one life substance, Deity, exists consciously as three persons.

This doctrine of the Trinity is the key to many of the teachings which concern the salvation of man. If God is not triune, Jesus Christ would not be God. Without the fact of the Trinity, the Christian could never really celebrate Christmas, for there would be no real incarnation (God in the flesh). If God is not triune, the Holy Spirit would not be God. What would happen then to the strengthening and abiding presence of God in our lives?

The Biblical teaching of the Trinity is no luxury for a few "deep thinkers" who love to juggle ideas. It is the keystone of the whole building of Christian truth. Although the Christian cannot explain this mysterious depth of God's Trinitarian life, he confesses this truth as the foundation of his Christianity. The sinner saved by Christ lives in dynamic fellowship with the one God who is Father, Son, and Holy Spirit. The Christian's God is great and greatly to be praised.

1. God is one in __________ and three in __________.
2. If one denies the doctrine of the Trinity, he would logically have to deny the __________ and the presence of the __________ __________ in our lives.

An Important Question

The Christian is often asked, "How do you know you are right? There are many conflicting views about God, man, sin, Christ, and salvation. Are they all equally correct? If only your views are right, how do you know for sure?" Such persistent questions deserve an honest answer.

In answering we follow the lead given by Christ Himself. He gave content to His views and supported His claims by using the Holy Scriptures. When Peter tried to prevent the Lord from going to the cross, our Savior appealed to the Word of God in the Old Testament, saying, "But how then should the Scriptures be fulfilled, that it must be so?" (Matt. 26:54). When the scribes, the experts in understanding the Old Testament, challenged the Lord's claim to be God's Son, Christ appealed to God's Word in Psalm 82:6. The Word of God was Christ's last court of appeal, His final authority.

The basis for conviction about Christian truth is the Bible. The standard by which we measure the content of faith is God's Holy Word. The Holy Writings are the final authority. We know for sure because God says so.

The Bible

The word *Bible* means "Book." It is the biggest little library in the world. It is divided into two testaments. All the books written before Jesus was born are called the Old Testament. All the books written after His birth are called the New Testament.

The Old Testament contains thirty-nine books and the New Testament twenty-seven.

These books are called God's Word, meaning that it is the word of which God Himself is the author. It is the word which He speaks. Just as your words originate from yourself, the Word of God comes from God. God's Word, the Bible, is inspired, that is, "God-breathed." God so worked in the minds and lives of the Bible writers that they wrote down God's thoughts and words. The product of their pens is a divine product.

That is why the Bible is infallible. The original writings as recorded in the Hebrew and Aramaic (Old Testament) and Greek (New Testament) languages are free from error. Every thought, idea, and word is true. We are sure of this because God's authorship lies behind the human writers. He controlled their hearts, heads, and hands. What God says is unalterably true. "God is not man that he should lie . . ." (Num. 23:19).

1. The __________ is the Christian's final authority for truth.
2. We say God wrote the Bible because He __________ the hearts, hands, and minds of its authors.
3. The Old Testament, written originally in __________ and __________, and the New Testament, written originally in __________, are true and free from error or __________.

The Bible Claims to Be God's Word

Throughout the entire Bible God testifies that He is speaking and writing. There are approximately two thousand places in the Old Testament where we read the phrase "Thus saith the Lord," or a phrase like it. God signs His own name to these thoughts, ideas, and words. These writings warrant belief just because they come from God.

Look closely how Jesus Christ used the Scriptures as God's own word. Listen to Him as He replied to Satan during His temptations in the wilderness. When tempted to turn stones into bread, He answered, "It is written, 'Man shall not live by bread alone, but by every word that proceeds from the mouth of God.' " When the devil urged Christ to jump from the pinnacle of the temple the Lord answered, "Again it is written, 'You shall not tempt the Lord your God.' " When Satan urged Christ to bow down to Him, the Master answered, "Begone, Satan! for it is written, 'You shall worship the Lord your God, and him only shall you serve' " (Matt. 4:3-10). The Bible regulated the life of our Lord. Jesus refused to do anything which contradicted the Bible. He was convinced it was the very Word of God.

When our Lord's enemies challenged His claim to be God's Son, He turned to the Bible and said, ". . . scripture cannot be broken" (John 10:35). Eagerly He walked the way of conduct laid down in the Bible. In the Sermon on the Mount He said, "Think not that I have come to abolish the law and the prophets; I have come not to abolish them but to fulfill them. For truly, I say to you, till heaven and earth pass away, not an iota, not a dot, will pass from the law until all is accomplished" (Matt. 5:17, 18). Because the Master viewed the law, the prophets, and the psalms as God's Word, He patterned His life to its claims.

Paul, the church's first great missionary, believed as Jesus did. Paul said, "All scripture is inspired by God and profitable for teaching, for reproof, for correction, and for training in righteousness . . . " (II Tim. 3:16). As one of the Bible writers, he knew that the Holy Spirit was directing his words, and thus he could claim that his words were God's words. "When you received the word of God which you heard from us, you accepted it not as the word of men, but as what it really is, the word of God . . ." (I Thess. 2:13). Remember this: Paul's writings cover about one half of the New Testament!

1. Both ____________ and ____________ repeatedly state that the Bible is God's own Word.
2. Paul who wrote more than ____________ ____________ of the New Testament claimed that his words were God's words.

The Testimony of the Holy Spirit

Many people, however, do not accept this claim of the Bible to be God's inspired Word. They view the Bible writings as purely human. They think the Bible is subject to all the limitations of error and insight common to man. These people act as judges of God's Word. They reject what does not fit into the pattern of their minds. They accept only what agrees with their views.

This fact underscores the need for a special work of the Holy Spirit. Before anyone will bow to the authority of the Bible he must be worked on by God. This work is called the testimony of the Holy Spirit. In this work God opens the Christian's mind to the evidences in the Bible which point to its divine authority. God opens the Christian's ear so that he hears the Bible message as God's own speech. Christ's sheep hear and recognize His voice (John 10).

All men are naturally sinful. They are inclined to resist God's will as made known in the Bible. "The unspiritual man does not receive the gifts of the Spirit of God, for they are folly to him, and he is not able to understand them because they are spiritually discerned" (I Cor. 2:14). Sin-power makes life and its meaning revolve around ourselves. We need this special work of the Holy Spirit to break through this limited circle of our self-centered views. When God breaks through our self-centered worlds, our hearts and minds are opened up to God's Word. This is what Jesus had in view when He said, "Unless one is born anew, he cannot see the Kingdom of God" (John 3:3). God must break into our world before we can be convinced that the Bible is God's inspired Word.

Think of an artist. With his sensitive eye he catches the austere beauty of the lonely pine. The artistically insensitive see the same tree but no beauty. Or think of a musician. With his sensitive ear he hears the symmetry and harmony of the score. The musically illiterate have the same sound waves strike their ears but hear only a confusion of noise. God must give us the eyes and ears to see and hear the Bible as His Word.

Therefore we approach the Holy Writings in the attitude of prayer. We need God's work in our lives. With the writer of the Psalms we pray, "Open my eyes, that I may behold wondrous things out of thy law" (Ps. 119:18).

1. Before the sinner will bow to the authority of the Bible, he must receive the __________ of the Holy Spirit in his heart.

LESSON 2

God Cares for His World

Biblical Facts About Beginnings

God does not need this world. God made it because He wants to display His glory. The whole universe is the product of God's will. First, God made the heavens and the earth, that is, the whole universe. Then He proceeded to order, arrange, and fit everything together into a meaningful whole.

This ordering is taught in the story of the six days of creation as recorded in Genesis 1. God made light. Then He made a firmament and separated the waters above from the waters below. On the third day God separated the waters and the dry land. Then God made the light-bearers in the heavens serviceable for the earth. On the fifth day God made the fish and fowl. On the sixth day God created animals and man. The seventh day was a day of rest.

The six-day interval of creation has been interpreted by Bible-believing scholars in different ways. Some believe that these days were literal days of twenty-four hours each. Others claim that some or all of these days may have been long periods and not ordinary days of twenty-four hours. However, they all believe that Genesis 1 does record what God actually did in originating man and his world.

At this point we must remember some very important Biblical facts, while at the same time allowing for some differences of interpretation of Genesis 1 and 2. First, creation is a specific act of God's will. In the whole process of creation nothing was left to blind chance. Second, God made man and his world in an orderly, systematic fashion. Third, God used some processes in the work of ordering and creating our world. Fourth, God definitely stopped His work of creation at a certain time and rested from His creation works. Fifth, man as God's image is definitely the crown and king of creation.

1. Creation is a specific act of God's __________, not the result of chance.
2. Creation was systematic, used processes, and God __________ on the seventh day.

Man, the Crown of Creation

God took special care in creating man. We read, "Then God said, 'Let us make man in our image and after our likeness' " (Gen. 1:26). This solemn declaration of God makes us pause. Man is a unique creature.

He is God's image. An image of someone is a reflection, a likeness, a certain type of representation. An image is seen on a photograph or in a statue. God made man to be an earthly, creaturely reflection of God Himself. God created man to be His representative on this earth. He endowed man with certain unique qualities. These special qualities help man in his task of representing God and reflecting God on earth.

Man had true knowledge of God. With this knowledge and insight man was made to act wisely and declare God's praise. Man had a perfectly sinless life in Paradise. He was holy. Man and God lived on terms of peace. Man was righteous. This is the way God made man. With these special gifts man was made to serve, honor, and praise God.

For this reason God set man to work in Paradise. God gave our first parents this command: "Be fruitful and multiply, and fill the earth and subdue it; and have dominion over the fish of the sea and over the birds of the air, and over every living thing that moves upon the earth" (Gen. 1:28). God made man to rule over this created universe.

As we shall learn later, man, the sinner, lost these unique qualities. Man's knowledge of God is now twisted, confused, and perverted. Sinfulness took the place of holiness. See Romans 1:18-23, 28-32. God and unsaved man now live in terms of alienation and wrath. In another sense, man is still God's image. He still tries to live as the crown of creation. But man in his sin is doomed to failure. He needs the salvation earned by Christ to regain his original dignity and destiny. Precisely because God made man so glorious in His image, He also sent His Son to save sinful man and restore him to the image of God.

1. Man was created in the image of God, and possessed true __________ of God, __________, and __________.

Creation, Man, and God's Companionship

God not only created man; He also decided to live in terms of friendship and companionship with man and creation. God made an arrangement with man in Paradise. This arrangement is called a covenant. In this covenant God laid down a condition of personal and perfect obedience. Man was not to eat of a special tree in the garden of Eden. This tree was called the "tree of the knowledge of good and evil" (Gen. 2:17). God threatened man with a death penalty if he disobeyed. "For in the day you eat of it you shall die" (Gen. 2:17).

God wanted man to live as His friend and companion. The road along which God's abiding friendship and love was to be enjoyed was the road of believing obedience. Man was to obey God just because God is God. Man was expected to take God at His word. As long as man did this, man and the whole of creation which was subject to man would continue to enjoy the loving presence of God. As long as man continued to obey and serve God, he lived in the presence of the Tree of Life.

Because of this arrangement the first man, Adam, is called a *public* person or a *representative* person. Adam was put in the position of acting for every other human being that was to be born. If he continued in the ways of obedient faith, all mankind would have continued to live in perfect harmony and friendship with God.

But we know now that Adam did not. He failed. He sinned and in him we sinned also. The first covenant in Paradise was broken. Man and creation were separated from God. They were cursed by God for the disobedience of man. But we must remember that everything in our world started beautifully. Man and creation were good. God delighted in them and called them "very good." Now God delights in man and creation because of the work of Jesus Christ our Lord. Our precious Savior restores man and the created world to abiding friendship with God. Christ Jesus is called the last Adam (I Cor. 15:45) because He took man's place and met all the stipulations of God's arrangement with Adam in Paradise.

1. In Paradise God made a __________ with man; the condition was __________ and the penalty was __________.
2. Adam, our __________ failed, resulting in the __________ between God and man.
3. The last Adam, __________, restores the __________ between God and man.

God's Providence

When God completed His work of creation He did not stop working. Every day He continues to take care of the universe which He made. This work is called divine providence.

God continues to preserve His creatures. Psalm 104:27 tells us that "These all look to thee, to give them their food in due season." In Acts 27:25 we read, "So take heart, men, for I have faith in God that it will be exactly as I have been told." God has placed the sand for a bound of the sea; "Do you not fear me? says the Lord; Do you not tremble before me? I placed the sand as the bound for the sea, a perpetual barrier which it cannot pass; though the waves toss, they cannot prevail, though they roar, they cannot pass over it." (Jer. 5:22). God works in such a way that every creature continues to live and serve a purpose for the honor of God's name.

In addition to preserving His creatures, God governs them. Not a sparrow falls to the ground without God's will (Matt. 10:29). Man proposes but God disposes. In Proverbs 16:9 we read, "A man's mind plans his way, but the Lord directs his steps." In the story of Joseph we read of his brothers' envy, greed, intent to kill, and final act of selling their brother into slavery. Later, Joseph confessed, "As for you, you meant evil against me; but God meant it for good, to bring it about that many people should be kept alive, as they are today" (Gen. 50:20). God governs everything from the hairs of man's head to actions of his life.

1. After completing His work of creation, God continued to __________ and __________ the universe.

God's Providence and God's Plan

God's work of preserving and governing all of creation proceeds according to His plan. There is nothing haphazard about this activity of providence. God worketh all things after the counsel of His will (Eph. 1:11). The solemn words of Isaiah 14:24 and 27 echo in our hearts: "The Lord of hosts has sworn: 'As I have planned, so shall it be, and as I have purposed, so shall it stand' . . . For the Lord of hosts has purposed, and who will annul it? His hand is stretched out, and who will turn it back?" The God and Father of our Lord Jesus Christ works according to the plan which He made before the world began.

Even evil and man's sin are included within this plan. Job, confident in his misery, exclaimed, "Shall we receive good at the hand of God, and shall we not receive evil?" (Job 2:10). When speaking of the crucifixion of the Savior, Peter declared under the inspiration of the Holy Spirit, "This Jesus, delivered up according to the definite plan and foreknowledge of God, you crucified and killed by the hands of lawless men" (Acts 2:23). The greatest of man's crimes, nailing God's only begotten Son to the cross, took place according to the plans and purpose of God.

As this fact of life dawns upon our consciousness we begin to understand the Preacher's words of Ecclesiastes 11:5, "As you do not know how the spirit comes to the bones in the womb of a woman with child, so you do not know the work of God who makes everything." The Christian bows in humble adoration before the wonders and the wisdom of his God.

1. God's incomprehensible plan includes ____________ as well as good.

God's Plan and Predestination

The word *predestination* refers to that part of God's plan which concerns the destiny of all sinners. This act involves the unconditional election of some to salvation, and the passing by and righteous condemnation of others.

The Bible's testimony is clear. Sinners are saved because God elected or chose them in Jesus Christ to walk the road of repentance and faith. In II Thessalonians 2:13 we read, "But we are bound to give thanks to God always for you, brethren beloved by the Lord, because God chose you from the beginning to be saved through sanctification by the Spirit and belief in the truth." Ephesians 1 teaches us that God "chose us in him [Christ] before the foundations of the world." God saved us "and called us with a holy calling, not in virtue of our works but in virtue of his own purpose and the grace which he gave us in Christ Jesus ages ago" (II Tim. 1:9). It is God's free and loving choice, unconditioned and uninfluenced by man's work, which determines man's salvation. Salvation is a gift of God, not of works, that no man should glory.

God passes others by. He leaves them in their sin. He is under no obligation to give them the gift of salvation. In abusing their freedom, they work themselves into the predicament of sin. And now God sovereignly decides not to give them the gift of grace. This is called reprobation. In addition to passing them by, God also condemns these sinners to their own just deserts according to His righteous judgment. "So then he has mercy upon whomever he wills, and he hardens the heart of whomever he wills" (Rom. 9:18). Peter tells us that some stumble at God's Word: "A stone that will make men stumble, a rock that will make them fall; for they stumble because they disobey the word, as they were destined to do" (I Peter 2:8). It is the will of God, not the will of man, which is determinative in the matter of man's final destiny. "For the Lord of hosts has purposed, and who will annul it? His hand is stretched out, and who will turn it back?" (Isa. 14:27).

At this point we do well to remember the words of Article 18 of the Canons of Dort. "To those who murmur at the free grace of election and the just severity of reprobation we answer with the apostle: 'But, who are you, a man, to answer back to God?' (Rom. 9:20) and quote the language of our Savior: 'Am I not allowed to do what I choose with what belongs to me? Or do you begrudge my generosity' (Matt. 20:15). And therefore, with holy adoration of these mysteries, we exclaim in the words of the apostle: 'O the depth of the riches and wisdom and knowledge of God! How unsearchable are his judgments and how inscrutable his ways! For who has known the mind of the Lord, or who has been his counselor? Or who has given a gift to him that he might be repaid? For from him and through him and to him are all things. To him be glory for ever. Amen' " (Rom. 11:33-36).

1. Predestination is that part of God's plan whereby he freely gives ____________ to some and passes others by.

Answering Objections

The Bible's teachings about God's everywhere-present activity in divine providence and God's all-inclusive and sovereign plan are objected to in various ways. Here are a few objections and their answers:

1. If God planned everything and controls everything, then God must be the author of sin. The Bible replies to this objection with emphasis: "Therefore, hear me, you men of understanding, far be it from God that he should do wickedness, and from the Almighty that he should do wrong" (Job 34:10). We are frank to admit that we cannot solve this problem of how God's actions are related to man's sinful actions. We do know that God is not the author of sin. God gives energy to His free creatures. He determines their actions in His own uniquely divine and mysterious manner. But it is man himself who gives to his actions their specific sinful quality. Man alone is responsible for the sinful quality of his deeds. Experience confirms this. Every sinner knows in his heart that he was never forced to sin. Whenever he thinks about sin he faces his own guilt.

2. Here is another objection: If God determines everything, then man's actions are not meaningful. This objection is met by considering that God determines not only the end results of life but also all the means which led to that final result. Think of Paul on the rudderless ship, about to crash on the reefs of the island of Melita (Acts 27). God determined that Paul and his shipmates were to come through alive. But Paul had to use the means. Paul told his fellow travelers not to abandon ship. He advised them to cling to floating boards or to swim. The means of swimming and clinging to the boards was part of the whole picture. All was controlled by God. God made man a responsible person. God urges, and even commands man to use the means at hand. Therefore, we use the means and leave everything safely in the hands of God. God determines the actions of His creatures in a way which underscores the full responsibility of the creature.

3. Let us consider one more objection: If God determined each man's destiny, then God does not and cannot freely offer salvation to all sinners and does not really want all sinners to repent and believe the gospel. However, Scripture is clear on this point: "Come to me, all who labor and are heavy-laden, and I will give you rest" (Matt. 11:28). "Ho, every one who thirsts, come to the waters" (Isa. 55:1). "Turn to me and be saved, all the ends of the earth!" (Isa. 45:22). "The Lord is not slow about his promise as some count slowness, but is forbearing toward you, not wishing that any should perish, but that all should

reach repentance" (II Peter 3:9). God takes no pleasure in the death of the wicked. He would have all men to be saved and come to the knowledge of the truth. God wants His servants to declare this gospel to the whole world. Even though we cannot logically harmonize God's plan to pass by some sinners with these texts which speak of God's full and free offer of salvation, we as humble believers accept the full teaching of God's Word.

These are just a few objections which men have raised against the teaching of God's Word. We must be careful to accept the *whole* teaching of the *whole* Bible even though we cannot fit everything together and figure it out with our minds. The genuine Christian bows before the authority of God's inspired and infallible Word. We worship a God who is greater than our minds, whose ways are beyond our comprehension. With Zophar we confess: "Can you find out the deep things of God? Can you find out the limit of the Almighty? It is higher than heaven—what can you do? Deeper than Sheol—what can you know? Its measure is longer than the earth, and broader than the sea" (Job 11:7-9).

1. Although we cannot completely understand God's plan, we may never conclude that God is the __________ of sin, that man's actions are meaningless, or that God desires the damnation of a segment of humanity.

LESSON 3

Enter the Enemy

There is an enemy of God. He sees the beauty of God's creation and hates it. Because he hates God, this enemy sets out to destroy God's work. At all costs he wants to drive a wedge between God and man.

The Enemy Identified

The enemy is Satan. His name means "adversary." He is also called the devil. This name means "accuser." There are many other titles given to him in the Bible. He is called the Dragon, the Evil One, the Prince of this World, the Angel of the Bottomless Pit, Belial, Beelzebub, the Prince of the Powers of the Air, the God of this World, Apollyon.

Satan is a fallen angel. We know very little about him before his fall into sin. Jude, verse 6, speaks of angels which have abandoned their proper sphere of activity. Rebellion against God appears to be the core of Satan's sin. The rebellious enemy continues to work evil with man and his world. This enemy possesses rare talents, power, and knowledge (Matt. 8:29; Mark 1:24). Christ Jesus called him a murderer from the beginning and the father of lies (John 8:44). Satan fired hatred toward Jesus and put treason into the heart of Judas (John 13:27). He is the chief of an army of evil spirits.

The Enemy's Strategy

The story of the devil's first invasion into man's world is found in Genesis 3. Adam and Eve, our first parents, listened to the lies of Satan. In Paradise the devil established his beachhead and ever since continues his clever work of destruction.

Satan twisted God's word. In this way he worked Eve and Adam into a position where they no longer believed God's word and obeyed it. It went like this:

God had given Adam a special command, "You may freely eat of every tree of the garden; but of the tree of the knowledge of good and evil you shall not eat, for in the day that you eat of it you shall die" (Gen. 2:16,17). God wanted to test man, His creature. God wanted man to obey His word without question, in freedom and joy. God gave this command for man's own good. As long as man walked the road of obedience, he would live in happy companionship with God.

"But the serpent said to the woman, 'You will not die. For God knows that when you eat of it your eyes will be opened, and you will be like God, knowing good and evil' " (Gen. 3:4, 5). In this way the father of lies schemed to make Eve doubt God's word. Once this seed of doubt was sown in her mind, the rest of the road to sin was easy. Eve then saw the tree, desired to eat its fruit because it appealed to her, and finally ate the fruit.

The enemy established his beachhead. Sin, disobedience to God's will, made its entry. Eve lured Adam into sin. Both of them then began to run away from God. They were ashamed of their nakedness. The beauty of their lives was changed to ugliness. The love in their lives was turned to shame. Their joy was lost and terror took its place.

Unbelief, refusing to take God at His word, lies at the root of all sin. Once Satan works sinners into a position where they let go of God's Word, he gains a big victory. This is the enemy's strategy. He still twists God's Word and makes it sound unjust and unreasonable. We must listen anew and afresh to God's Word. Only as we obediently accept God's Word can we escape the devil's wicked plans.

1. Satan, entering man's world in __________, twisted God's word, making it seem unjust.
2. __________ lies at the root of all sin.

God Is Not Mocked

"Do not be deceived" said Paul, "God is not mocked, for whatever a man sows, that he will also reap" (Gal. 6:7). Man sowed sin; he reaps God's righteous judgment. Moses knew this too. "God is not man, that he should lie, or a son of man, that he should repent. Has he said, and will he not do it? Or has he spoken and will he not fulfill it?" (Num. 23:19). In holy anger and righteous judgment the good and loving Creator keeps His word. He said, "In the day thou eatest thereof thou shalt surely die." And man died!

Man was cut off from God's loving companionship. This is *spiritual* death. Filled with fear, Adam and Eve hid from God. The first sinners hid among the trees of the garden (Gen. 3:8). Modern sons and daughters of Adam and Eve hide themselves in different ways. "Dead through trespasses and sins" (Eph. 2:1), they fearfully hide themselves and are unable to respond to God's loving search for them.

Man was cursed with *physical* death. "You are dust, and to dust you shall return" (Gen. 3:19). Every funeral procession seen on our streets is a grim testimony to the truth and righteousness of God. "Therefore as sin came into the world through one man and death through sin, and so death spread to all men because all men sinned" (Rom. 5:12).

The worst kind of death is *eternal* death. This is the final, unchangeable separation from God in the punishment of hell. This place of final punishment is described in the Bible by many symbols. Hell is the place of "unquenchable fire," "the blackness of darkness," "furnace of fire," "torment in fire and brimstone," "where their worm dieth not," "the place prepared for the devil and his angels." It is the place of unspeakable misery and sorrow. It is the end of the road for all who do not believe on the Lord Jesus Christ.

Death in this threefold sense is the wages of sin. It is this kind of death, justly deserved by sinners like ourselves, which Jesus died for sinners. "If, because of one man's trespass, death reigned through that one man, much more will those who receive the abundance of grace and the free gift of righteousness reign in life through the one man Jesus Christ" (Rom. 5:17). God does not leave sin unpunished. He punishes it in the life of the sinner himself or in the life of the sin-bearer, Jesus Christ.

1. The punishment for sin is three-fold death.
   a. ____________ death cuts man off from God's friendship.
   b. ____________ death returns man to the dust.
   c. ____________ death is final separation from God in hell.

Adam, Eve, and You

What happened in Paradise concerns you; Adam and Eve were our first parents. From them we inherit our sinful natures; like begets like. As a parent you pass on certain physical traits to your children. Think of your child's blue eyes. So Adam and Eve passed on to us, their children, a sinful, selfish way of life. This is what we call inheriting the pollution or corruption of sin.

For this reason our children are born with a "me first" attitude toward life. Just watch them fight over their toys. In the light of this inheritance from our first parents, we can understand the "give me the biggest piece" attitude of so many in our world. A bad tree brings forth bad fruit. Jesus had this in mind when He said to Nicodemus, "That which is born of the flesh is flesh" (John 3:6). David, sadly thinking about his own sin, said, "Behold, I was brought forth in iniquity, and in sin did my mother conceive me" (Ps. 51:5).

But there is more. Adam was a public person; he represented us. God made an arrangement called a covenant with Adam. In his action of eating or not eating from the tree of the knowledge of good and evil, Adam was acting in our place, for us, for every human being. Just like our duly-elected senators represent us in the senate chambers, so God chose Adam to represent us in Paradise.

Because Adam was our representative, his guilt is reckoned to be our guilt. If one is elected as a senator and goes out and steals, his action reflects on the people who sent him to

Washington. People will say, "Those who elected him must be as dishonest as he. Otherwise they would not have chosen him." Adam's worthiness to be punished comes to us. Since he acted in our place, we are held chargeable with his sin. This truth is plainly taught in Romans 5 and in I Corinthians 15. In these chapters we read of a special comparison between Adam and Christ. Just as Adam acted for us, so Christ acted for sinners. It is this representation in Adam which brings sin into our lives. It is this representation in Christ which gives salvation in the way of faith. What happened in Paradise is important. It explains much about our sinful lives.

1. Just as we inherit physical traits from our ancestors, so we inherit our sinful natures from our first parents, Adam and Eve. This is called the __________ or __________ of sin.
2. Since Adam was our __________ in Paradise, his __________ is reckoned to be __________ guilt.

Our Present Predicament

We sinners are in a bad way. We are much worse off than we often imagine. Too many people fool themselves by thinking they are better in God's sight than they really are. The Bible speaks in clear language:

In Genesis 6:5 and 8:21, we read that the imagination of the thoughts of the heart of man is continuously evil, from his youth up. Jeremiah 17:9 tells us that "the heart is deceitful above all things and desperately corrupt." Paul pulls no punches in Romans 8:8, "Those who are in the flesh cannot please God." The mind of the unsaved sinner "does not submit to God's law, indeed it cannot" (Rom. 8:7). There is no mistaking the language of Romans 3:12, "All have turned aside, together they have gone wrong; no one does good, not even one." And all this describes you as you are in this world without the work of Jesus Christ.

This means that man is totally depraved. Every part of our lives is sinful. Our thoughts, our feelings, and our wills are perverted. Of course, man is not as bad as he could be. The Bible teaches us that some sinners do relatively good things. But this good is not pleasing to God. To be totally depraved means that there is not an area in our lives where we do a single work that is thoroughly pleasing to God. Without Christ we are dead in trespasses and sins, completely unable and unwilling to please God.

Such a fact must be faced. At this point we cannot argue with God or present our excuses. Sinners must stop whistling in the dark, acting as if life is not as bad as the Bible says it is. We must learn to pray as the publican prayed in the temple. He hardly dared to lift his eyes heavenward. Brokenhearted, he prayed, "God, be merciful to me a sinner." Of this man who admitted his guilt, Jesus said, he "went down to his house justified rather than the other . . . . he who humbles himself will be exalted" (Luke 18:14).

1. Total depravity means that man as sinner is __________ to do anything __________ pleasing to God.

LESSON 4

The Great Substitution

Adam failed, but God did not abandon the sinner to the power of sin. God declared war against the enemy, providing a way out. This good news was first declared in Genesis 3:15, "I will put enmity between you and the woman, and between your seed and her seed; he shall bruise your head, and you shall bruise his heel." This "seed of the woman" is Jesus Christ our Lord. He is the Christian's substitute. He came to do what we were unable to do and unwilling to do.

Like As We Are

God's substitute for sinners is a man. Jesus was and is today as human as we are. He was born of the Virgin Mary. He took His flesh and blood from His blessed mother. He lived a normal childhood. "And Jesus increased in wisdom and in stature, and in favor with God and man" (Luke 2:52). After a hard day's work He was tired and hungry. When His friend Lazarus died Jesus wept (John 11:34, 35). In the presence of sin Jesus became angry (Luke 3:7). He "has been tempted as we are, yet without sinning" (Heb. 4:15).

This full manhood of the Master is an important fact. We humans are sinful, " . . .Since all have sinned and fall short of the glory of God" (Rom. 3:23). Man must pay for his own sins. "For the wrongdoer will be paid back for the wrong he has done, and there is no partiality" (Col. 3:25). "The soul that sins shall die" (Ezek. 18:4). Our holy and just God demands this. Now, in perfect agreement with His own holiness and justice, God sent a substitute who is completely human. God's work of salvation in Jesus is marvelous in our eyes. He sent a Savior suited to our needs, and perfectly fitted to take our place.

1. After Adam sinned, God provided a ________, Jesus Christ, who was, and is completely ________.

The Son of God

Jesus is more than a man. He is the eternal God manifest in the flesh. Our substitute testified under oath that He was the Son of God. In court Jesus was asked, "Are you the Son of God, then?" Calmly He said unto them, "You say that I am" (Luke 22:70). Jesus left no doubt in the minds of His listeners when He said, "I and the Father are one" (John 10:30). God Himself testified that Jesus was His Son. It happened on the Mount of Transfiguration: "And a voice came out of the cloud, saying, 'This is my Son, my Chosen; listen to him.' " (Luke 9:35). Paul also states it plainly, "For in him the whole fulness of deity dwells bodily" (Col. 2:9).

In giving sinners a *divine* substitute, God displays His love and wisdom. Only God Himself can work salvation for us. The debt of death we must pay is eternal. A mere man would take forever to complete this payment. If man were left to earn his own salvation, he would never finish his work. An eternal debt requires an eternity to pay. Knowing our pitiful situation God sent His only begotten Son as our substitute. Jesus Christ is the God-man, perfectly suited to take our place. Truly, a wonderful Savior is Jesus our Lord.

1. Since a ________ substitute could never pay an eternal debt, our Savior would have to be divine also.
2. The only possible substitute then would have to be Jesus Christ, who would be both ________ and ________.

The Work of Our Substitute

To understand the work of Christ Jesus we must understand who we are. We are *creatures*; that is first. We are *sinful* creatures; that is second. Both of these facts tell us the secret of Jesus' work.

As *creatures* we are completely dependent upon God and subject to His law. To be a creature means to be subject to law. God's law is for the creature what oxygen is for our lungs and what water is for a fish. God's law is the atmosphere of man's life. We live happily only as we willingly obey God's law.

As *sinful* creatures we are exposed to the penalties of God's law. He who breaks the law will be broken by the law. In the last lesson we learned what the Bible teaches about the punishments of God. As sinners we must bear these punishments.

Jesus came into this situation. "God sent forth his Son, born of woman, born under the law . . . so that we might receive adoption as sons" (Gal. 4:5). Jesus Christ did what we as sinful creatures were supposed to do. He obeyed God's law in all things for us. The Lord Himself said, "For I have come down from heaven, not to do my own will, but the will of him who sent me . . ." (John 6:38). Paul puts the matter plainly, "For as by one man's disobedience many were made sinners, so by one man's obedience many will be made righteous" (Rom. 5:19). Our substitute obeyed for us in two ways:

1. Our Savior paid the penalties which we sinners deserved. Sinners deserve sorrow. "Surely he has borne our griefs and carried our sorrows" (Isa. 53:4). Sin itself is often a punishment for sin. Think of the arsonist or the murderer. "And the Lord has laid on him the iniquity of us all" (Isa. 53:6). "For our sake he made him to be sin who knew no sin, so that in him we might become the righteousness of God" (II Cor. 5:21). Sinners are worthy of God's curse. "Christ redeemed us from the curse of the law, having become a curse for us" (Gal. 3:13). We deserve death, "but God shows his love for us in that while we were yet sinners Christ died for us" (Rom. 5:8). The Good Shepherd laid down His life for the sheep (John 10:15). Jesus the Lamb of God, our great High Priest, paid our penalty. Every punishment we sinners deserve was carried away by the sin-bearer.

2. Jesus also gave to God the willing obedience which we owed to God. He obeyed every commandment for us. He discharged every duty for us. This also was a big part of His work. God's Son "learned obedience through what he suffered; and

being made perfect he became the source of eternal salvation to all who obey him" (Heb. 5:8, 9).

Every step of His life Jesus took obediently. As a child He went down to Nazareth with His parents "and was obedient to them" (Luke 2:51). He obeyed the details of God's law in the ceremony of baptism: "Let it be so now; for thus it is fitting for us to fulfil all righteousness" (Matt. 3:15). When He healed a leper He instructed the leper to the law, saying, "Go, show yourself to the priest, and offer for your cleansing what Moses commanded, for a proof to the people" (Mark 1:44). Humbling Himself as our substitute He was "obedient unto death, even death on a cross" (Phil. 2:8). He practiced what He preached: "Think not that I have come to abolish the law and the prophets; I have come not to abolish them but to fulfil them" (Matt. 5:17).

In this way of obedience to every detail of God's law, Jesus earned perfect salvation for us. Jesus now freely gives us a title to eternal life. Sinners who put the full weight of their lives on this Savior become with Jesus "heirs of God and fellow heirs with Christ" (Rom. 8:17).

1. Humans are __________, and thus are subject to the law. As __________ creatures humans are also subject to the __________ of the law.
2. Christ obeyed the law for us in two ways: He paid the __________. He __________ every commandment for us. Thus He earned __________ for us.

A Definite Substitution

The work of our substitute was carried out according to God's plan. It is a definite work which included a special number of sinners. From all eternity God planned to save certain people, not every human being in the world. Everyone for whom Christ substituted Himself shall be saved.

Some people think that Jesus worked only in order to give people a chance to be saved. They reason: Jesus did His part in the work of salvation for every sinner on earth. Now it is up to the sinner. He must either accept or reject the work of Christ. In other words, Jesus is now dependent on the sinner. As a substitute He did all there was to do. Now He must wait for the sinner to make up his mind. However, this is not the Biblical presentation.

The Biblical presentation states that Jesus substituted Himself for the elect, for those whom the Father had given Him (John 17:11). Jesus Himself said, "The good shepherd lays down his life for the sheep" (John 10:11). He loved the church and gave Himself up for it. Jesus substituted Himself for the elect, for those who were chosen in Him before the foundation of the world.

If this were not true, Jesus' work as a substitute would have been a failure. Think of this: There are more sinners who do not believe in Him as Savior than there are sinners who do believe. If Jesus obeyed and worked as a substitute for every human being, then He must have failed. Most sinners ignore Him and refuse to serve Him.

Worse still, if Jesus worked as a substitute for everyone, then God would be unjust in sending sinners into eternal condemnation. Obviously, many are going to hell. The Bible is clear on this point. But if Jesus as their substitute paid the penalty and earned salvation for them, then God would not send them to hell. God is supremely just. He would never allow Jesus to pay the price for a man's sin and yet condemn that man.

Christ Jesus earned perfect salvation, complete in every detail. He substituted Himself for a definite number. You can be sure He worked for you only as you believe and trust Him for your salvation. He opened your heart and filled you with the longing to know Him better and love Him more. Believe on the Substitute and you will be saved. As you believe, you know that He worked as *your* substitute.

At first glance it may seem that the teaching of a definite substitution is a harsh doctrine. A little thought, however, after a second glance at this teaching, shows something quite different. This is a warm and comforting teaching. It means Jesus Christ worked effectively for me while on earth. Right now He is continuing to carry out His program unto perfection. He does not merely give me a chance to be saved. He gives something much different, something much more needful and wonderful. Christ saves all the way. He redeems to the uttermost. He fully and completely secures the final salvation of believers. The sheep for whom He substituted Himself shall certainly be saved.

Our Great Shepherd said, "My sheep hear my voice, and I know them, and they follow me; and I give them eternal life, and they shall never perish, and no one shall snatch them out of my hand" (John 10:27, 28). Just imagine the haunting fear and uncertainty which would plague our lives if Jesus had said, "I give my sheep a chance for eternal life; and maybe they will never perish if they continue to do their part in the work of salvation." Thank God, Jesus never said anything like that. Our part in the work of salvation would never be given.

Thus Christ does it all. And the works we must perform are achieved only because Christ constantly gives His energizing grace unto His sheep. So we rejoice in the comforting truth that Jesus worked effectively for all those sheep whom the Father in heaven had given unto Him. And our Lord lovingly urges all men everywhere to share in His accomplished work in the way of repentance and faith.

1. God planned to save only the ____________, not every human being in the world. If this were not true, part of Christ's work would have been a ____________, and God would be unjust in condemning any for whom Christ had already earned ____________.
2. The comfort of believing in a definite ____________ is that ____________ did it all.

LESSON 5

The Victorious Lord

Jesus of Nazareth is now the victorious Lord. The One born in Bethlehem's manger, the One who walked the dusty roads of Palestine, the One who died as a criminal on Calvary, is the reigning Lord of Glory. God rewarded our obedient substitute: "Therefore God has highly exalted him and bestowed on him the name which is above every name" (Phil. 2:9).

Victory Over Death

Jesus stayed in His grave three days. On Easter Sunday morning God raised Him from the dead. Death could not keep Him. Christ tore the bars away. Because our Savior obeyed fully and completely God rewarded Him. God raised Him up, "having loosed the pangs of death, because it was not possible for him to be held by it" (Acts 2:24). The power of death was broken. You can read the accounts of this miracle in the four Gospels (Matt. 28; Mark 16; Luke 24; John 20).

Christ defeated death; this is the Christian's comfort. Our substitute went into the grave to remove its terrors. The great enemy—death—need not frighten the Christian. To be sure, Christians die. But their souls go to be with Jesus in the glories of heaven (Phil. 1:23; Luke 23:43). Their bodies, gently laid to rest in the grave, are seeds in the earth. In the day of the resurrection these seeds shall be raised unto power and glory (I Cor. 15:35-49). The believing Christian sorrows, but he does not sorrow without hope. The words of Revelation 14:13 strengthen the sorrowing: "Blessed are the dead who die in the Lord henceforth." In this nuclear age the Christian can look death in the face without fear, declaring, "O death, where is thy victory? O death, where is thy sting?" (I Cor. 15:55).

1. Since Christ defeated death, the Christian need no longer be ____________ of dying.

The Ruling King

Forty days after Jesus broke the bars of death He went into heaven. God gave Him the right to enter into glory. While He blessed His faithful disciples Jesus ascended before their very eyes. He was seen by them until a cloud received Him from their sight (Luke 24:50, 51; Acts 1:6-11).

Jesus was given the highest honor of heaven: "The Lord says to my lord: 'Sit at my right hand, till I make your enemies your footstool' " (Ps. 110:1). The phrase, "the right hand of God" is not to be taken literally. God is a Spirit. He has no body, no right hand. The phrase means that Jesus Christ is now enjoying the highest honor. Saved saints in heaven and holy angels worship Him, saying, "Worthy art thou, our Lord and God, to receive glory and honor and power" (Rev. 4:11).

This victorious Lord now works for God's glory and our salvation. This fact of faith gives new strength for life, new purpose, and new meaning for every experience of every day. The ruling King concerns Himself with our lives.

Christ continues to teach us God's will as our *Chief Prophet*. He sends the Holy Spirit to lead the church into all truth (John 16:13). From His throne in glory Christ sends to His people apostles, prophets, evangelists, and teachers (Eph. 4:11). Jesus continues to light up the road of life with the knowledge of the will of God. In this age of confusion our great teacher continues to direct our footsteps homeward to our eternal rest.

Jesus continues to pray for us as our *only* High Priest. He entered "not into a sanctuary made with hands, a copy of the true one, but into heaven itself, now to appear in the presence of God on our behalf" (Heb. 9:24). He sees each tear we shed. He knows each temptation we face. He understands each fear within the soul. "Is it Christ Jesus, who died, yes, who was raised from the dead, who is at the right hand of God, who indeed intercedes for us?" (Rom. 8:34). As we look to Jesus we experience the peace of God which "passeth all understanding." He makes our daily cares His concern. With infinite tenderness He watches over those who belong to Him. He makes His sacrifice for sins effective in our lives.

Our substitute works for us as the *Eternal King*. Everything, from the lines on our faces to the leaders of the world, is under the control of Christ. Our King makes everything serve the saved. God "put all things under his feet and has made him the head over all things to the church" (Eph. 1:22). "To the church" means for the sake of the believing sinner. Our nuclear age holds frightening possibilities for evil. With Christ as our King we know that not a missile can be launched or a bomb dropped without His will. As our lives focus on Christ's Kingship we live as more than conquerors.

The Eternal King also controls all our enemies. Just before He went to heaven He said, "All authority in heaven and on earth has been given to me" (Matt. 28:18). The Christian's enemies attack and counterattack, but they cannot win the battle for our souls. Our enemies are many: They are our own sinful tendencies to selfishness. There is the Christ-less world organized to do evil. There is Satan, the enemy supreme (I Peter 5:8-11). These enemies cannot harm us. "For he [Christ] must reign until he has put all his enemies under his feet" (I Cor. 15:25). It is the saved sinner, trusting fully in his substitute, who can live in poise and peace in our troubled world. Even the evils of life are under the perfect control of our reigning Savior.

1. After Christ's __________ into heaven, He continued to work for us in a three-fold way:
   a. As our __________ __________ He teaches us God's will.
   b. As our __________ __________ __________ He prays and intercedes for us.
   c. As our __________ __________ He controls every aspect of our lives.

The Lord's Return

Christ always keeps His word. He promised to return. He will come again to finish the work He began while He lived in

Palestine and which He carries on today. His coming again is the climax of His victory. "Then will appear the sign of the Son of man in heaven, and then all the tribes of the earth will mourn, and they will see the Son of man coming on the clouds of heaven with power and great glory . . ." (Matt. 24:30).

We do not know the time of His return. "But of that day or that hour no one knows, not even the angels in heaven, nor the Son, but only the Father" (Mark 13:32). God does not want His children to pry curiously into the exact time. The Christians, however, must read the signs which Christ gives. Daily events reported in newspapers and on television should be seen in the light of our Lord's return. Jesus Himself mentioned various signs which herald His return:

1. The preaching of the gospel to all nations (Matt. 24:14).
2. The return of the Jews to Christ (Rom. 11:25, 26).
3. The appearance of many false teachers who shall work miracles, deceiving many (Mark13:22).
4. Signs in the world of nature and nations. Wars and rumors of wars; famine; earthquakes and signs in the sky (Luke 21:25-27).
5. The coming of the Anti-Christ (II Thess. 2:3; I John 2:18).

Many of these signs are seen today. They are taking place with greater power and on a bigger scale than ever before. Our earth ball, shrunken by mass communication, has become a feasible matrix for the coming of the Anti-Christ. As the Christian sees these things and thinks about them, he hears the footsteps of the coming Savior. When Christ will come we do not know. But when He comes it will be wonderful for the Christian.

When our victorious Lord returns, a number of big events shall take place in our lives. These big happenings are all clustered around the final return of Jesus. At His coming in power and great glory the following events will take place:

1. There will be the *resurrection of the dead*. "The hour is coming when all who are in the tombs will hear his voice and come forth, those who have done good, to the resurrection of life, and those who have done evil, to the resurrection of judgment" (John 5:28, 29). This is comforting for the Christian and terrifying for those who do not know Jesus as Savior and Lord.

2. There will be the *rapture*. This means that when Jesus comes again He will bring with Himself the souls of the saved

in heaven. These souls will be reunited quickly, in the twinkling of an eye, with their resurrection bodies. When their souls are joined with their bodies they go forth to meet Christ in the air. The rapture is a coming of Christ with His saints (souls) and for the saints (souls joined with their new bodies). Then shall dawn the thrill of full salvation, a joy unspeakable and full of glory. ". . . And so we shall always be with the Lord" (I Thess. 4:13-18). What a joy to anticipate!

3. There will be the *final judgment* (Rev. 20:11-15). All shall appear before the great throne. Then Christ shall make a final, a public, an everlasting separation between the sheep and the goats (Matt. 25:31-46). Believers shall be given glory and unbelievers shall be cast into the pit of everlasting condemnation. It will be the time of eternal joy for the saved and a time of eternal sorrow for the unsaved.

4. Finally, there will be a *new heaven and a new earth*. This present universe shall be refined, purified with fire (II Peter 3:7-12). Out of the ashes of the old will arise a new world. "But according to his promise we wait for new heavens and a new earth in which righteousness dwells" (II Peter 3:13). Something of the rare beauty and glory of this new world is described in Revelation 21 and 22.

Christ is working toward that final day right now. The happenings of world history are alive with the unseen but real movements of the Spirit of Christ Jesus. Our Savior is going to save the world. The time is coming when God shall be perfectly honored and praised in a perfect world by a perfect people. Christ shall accomplish this. Then—O the mystery of divine salvation—God Himself shall be all and in all (I Cor. 15:28). We Christians shall understand perfectly: "For from him and through him and to him are all things. To him be glory forever. Amen" (Rom. 11:36). This final day is one for which the Christian longs. It will be the day of full salvation for the sinner and the day of full praise to God. Let us live with our feet planted firmly in the soil of daily events and our eyes of faith looking forward to the coming of our victorious Lord.

1. Although we do not know the exact time of Christ's ___________ the observant Christian can detect many signs that this will occur.

2. At the time of Christ's return there will be a __________ of the dead, a __________ which is the reunion of the saved souls in heaven with their resurrection bodies, a final __________, and the arising of a new __________ and a new __________ out of the ashes of the old.

LESSON 6

The Life-Giving Christ

Every sinner needs living contact with Jesus Christ the Substitute. The Savior is in heaven. The sinner is on earth. When these two come into personal companionship there is personal salvation. God the Holy Spirit brings these two together. This is the chief work of the Holy Spirit. This work of the life-giving Spirit displays the wonder of God's grace in the work of salvation. Every need of the sinner is fully met by the provisions of God—the Father, the Son, and the Holy Spirit.

The Spirit Poured Out

Ten days after Jesus went into heaven He sent the Holy Spirit. On Pentecost day about 120 believers were praying and waiting for their Master to send the other comforter. He had promised not to leave them as orphans in the world (John 14:18). Suddenly, without warning, God the Holy Spirit came. A new, a strange, a wonderful power took hold of them. "And they were all filled with the Holy Spirit . . ." (Acts 2:4). Then the waiting, praying disciples went into action. They declared the mighty works of God, and as they preached, thousands of sinners were given new life. God the Holy Spirit gave them a new birth, a birth from above. About three thousand people were saved in one day.

Peter explained this miracle for his hearers. He pointed the people to Jesus: "This Jesus God raised up, and of that we all are witnesses. Being therefore exalted at the right hand of God, and having received from the Father the promise of the Holy Spirit, he has poured out this which you see and hear" (Acts 2:32, 33). The victorious Lord Jesus sent forth the Holy Spirit. It is the Holy Spirit who connects the sinner with Jesus the Savior.

The Holy Spirit is God. He is the third person of the Trinity and is as fully God as are the Father and Son. He is a person, not only a power or influence. A person can lie to the Holy Spirit (Acts 5:3, 4). The sinner can grieve the Holy Spirit (Eph. 4:30). A person cannot lie to or grieve a mere power. This can only be done to a person. We also read that the Holy Spirit gives gifts to sinners (I Cor. 12:11). It is a fact; the Holy Spirit is a divine person. When He comes into the life of a sinner to save him, this means that God Himself comes into that life.

1. The chief work of God the Holy Spirit is to bring the __________ and the __________ into personal contact.
2. The Holy Spirit poured out on __________ is God, third person of the Trinity.

The Spirit and the Message

As soon as Jesus Christ sent forth the Holy Spirit, the disciples began to preach. They proclaimed fearlessly the work of Christ to all men. Obeying the instructions of Jesus, they began at Jerusalem in the temple. From this center they fanned out until they reached the boundaries of the Roman Empire. The exciting story of the growing Church is told by Luke in the Book of Acts. This church was a witnessing church.

As the disciples told the message, Jesus continued to save sinners (Acts 2:47). Peter and John preached in the temple "and more than ever believers were added to the Lord, multitudes both of men and women" (Acts 5:14). Philip, the Evangelist, preached in the country of Samaria "and the multitudes with one accord gave heed to what was said by Philip" (Acts 8:6). Paul traveled all over the known world. Women like Lydia (Acts 16:14), philosophers like Dionysius (Acts 17:34), and even members of Caesar's palace (Rom. 16) were saved. It was true then; it is true today. "For since, in the wisdom of God, the world did not know God through wisdom, it pleased God through the folly of what we preach to save those who believe" (I Cor. 1:21).

One fact must be remembered: Christ Jesus sends the Holy Spirit in connection with the gospel message and establishes living contact with the sinner. This is the first step on the road of personal salvation. Preachers explain many truths about God and man, sin and salvation. At the heart of their message is Jesus Christ and His wonderful work on behalf of sinners. As God's work in Christ is declared, the sinner is summoned to turn from sin and to trust in Jesus. "Believe in the Lord Jesus, and you will be saved, you and your household" (Acts 16:31).

Paul explained his work to King Agrippa as follows: "Wherefore, O King Agrippa, I was not disobedient to the heavenly vision, but declared first to those at Damascus, then at Jerusalem and throughout all the country of Judea, and also to the Gentiles, that they should repent and turn to God and perform deeds worthy of their repentance" (Acts 26:19, 20). In the name of Christ Jesus, on the authority of Christ Jesus, preachers urged sinners to repent and believe. This gospel call is the first step on the road to personal salvation.

1. Christ reaches sinners through the __________ of the gospel call which is the first step on the road to personal salvation.

Born Again

The Holy Spirit works through the message to give new life. The Christian has been "born anew, not of perishable seed but of imperishable, through the living and abiding word of God; for 'All flesh is like grass and all its glory like the flower of grass. The grass withers, and the flower falls, but the word of the Lord abides for ever.' That word is the good news which was preached to you" (I Peter 1:23–25). Every time the Word of God is preached and witnessed to by Christians, we pray that God may work the miracle of new life in the lives of those sinners still dead in sin. In the hands of the Holy Spirit the gospel preached is the power of God unto salvation.

The act of God by which He makes the spiritually dead sinner alive is called regeneration. God reaches down to the lowest depths of the sinner's need. A miracle takes place. A new life is given, which is called a new creation. This gift of regeneration is as marvelous, as astonishing, as indescribable as the creation of the world out of nothing.

This renewal—new creation, resurrection from the dead, making alive—takes place without our help. The sinner does not cooperate with God in this work. When we were born from our earthly parents we did not cooperate with our parents. In being born we were completely passive. So the sinner is passive when God makes him alive. God and His grace receive the honor and the praise alone.

The saved sinner becomes a new creature: "Therefore, if any one is in Christ, he is a new creation; the old has passed away, behold, the new has come" (II Cor. 5:17). The born-again sinner thinks differently. He begins to think God's thoughts. The regenerated sinner feels differently. His likes and dislikes change so that he loves the things of the Spirit. His will works differently. He decides to break with sin, believe on the Lord, and follow the Master. The dead sinner made-alive listens to God's Word and the gospel message. He now begins to pattern his life according to the truth of God.

1. The Holy Spirit uses the preached gospel message to create the miracle of __________ in the spiritually dead sinner.
2. Just as a baby is passive in his physical birth, so the sinner is passive in his __________ birth.
3. The saved sinner becomes a __________ creature, thinking and acting according to __________ will.

Repentance

John the Baptist prepared the way for the coming of Christ. His message was "Repent and believe in the gospel" (Mark

1:15). Jesus Himself preached this message: "Repent for the kingdom of heaven is at hand" (Matt. 4:17). Paul followed the example of his Master. At Athens he said, "The times of ignorance God overlooked, but now he commands all men everywhere to repent, because he has fixed a day on which he will judge the world in righteousness by a man whom he has appointed . . ." (Acts 17:30-31). Repentance is an imperative. It is a command made to all. Obedience to His command flows from our new life.

In repentance we admit our sin. The Christian compares his life with the great commandment, "You shall love the Lord your God with all your heart, and with all your soul, and with all your mind. This is the great and first commandment. And a second is like it, You shall love your neighbor as yourself" (Matt. 22:37-39). The Christian learns to see his attitudes and actions as not measuring up to this law of love. He admits his sin as he swallows his pride. He confesses his sins and stops making excuses for himself. With David he says, "For I know my transgressions" (Ps. 51:3). With the publican in the temple the repentant sinner cries out, "God be merciful to me a sinner" (Luke 18:13).

In repentance we experience sorrow for our sins. This is the godly sorrow which "produces a repentance that leads to salvation" (II Cor. 7:10). This is not a mere regret because one must accept punishment. Judas, the betrayer, had his regrets, but no godly sorrow. True sorrow for sin is born out of love for God. The new-born sinner has experienced God's love in Jesus Christ. Every time the Christian sins he is sorry that he has wounded the love of God. And so he turns away from sinful actions.

Faith

When a person turns *from* something he must turn *to* something. The sinner does exactly that. He turns from sin to holiness, from self to the Savior. Repentance is the *turning from* and faith is the *turning to*. Repentance and faith are the two sides of one coin.

To believe in someone involves knowing the person in whom you have faith. One part of faith is "a sure knowledge, whereby I hold for truth all that God has revealed to us in his word"

(Heidelberg Cathechism, Answer 21). The truth in the Bible about God, ourselves, sin, and the Savior must become convictions in our lives. The knowledge of faith knows with conviction the truths of Scripture.

To believe in someone also involves trust. This is another part of faith. Faith is "a firm confidence which the Holy Spirit works in my heart by the gospel, that not only to others, but to me also, remission of sins, everlasting righteousness and salvation are freely given by God" (Heidelberg Cathechism, Answer 21). This means self-surrender to Jesus Christ and his Word. Faith means no longer relying on self but complete reliance on the Savior. This is relying and resting upon Jesus Christ.

Both knowledge and confidence must penetrate each other. Our knowledge of Christ must be colored by full trust, and our full trust must be supported by knowledge. This faith is the empty hand which longs to be filled by God. To believe is to abandon ourselves completely to God and Jesus Christ.

1. When we truly repent we ____________ our sin and experience ____________ that we have grieved God whom we love.
2. Repentance is the turning from ____________, and the turning to ____________.
3. Faith is composed of knowledge of and ____________ in Christ.

Peace With God

The most important question of religion is: Am I right with God? The Christian knows he is a sinner. He also knows God is perfectly holy. The question becomes urgent: Am I, the unholy sinner, right with God, the Holy One?

This question is answered for the genuine believer. In the act of believing, the sinner rejoices in the good news of peace with God. He knows what Paul means in Romans 5:1, "Therefore, since we are justified by faith, we have peace with God through our Lord Jesus Christ." This is the heartbeat of the gospel. The guilty sinner is declared by the Holy God to be free from guilt. Instead of undergoing the condemnation he deserves, the believing sinner is justified. In the act of faith the sinner rejoices saying, "Who shall bring any charge against God's elect? It is God who justifies; who is to condemn?" (Rom. 8:33, 34). The sinner lives on terms of peace with God.

In justification the holy and righteous God declares the guilty sinner completely free from his sins. The godless sinner is declared godly. God the Judge does this in a way which fits in with His perfect holiness and righteousness. God takes the perfect work of Jesus Christ and reckons it to the believing sinner's life. God takes the whole work of our substitute and applies it to the believer's account. The Judge declares the work of the Savior to be the work of the believer.

Think of this miracle of free grace as something like this: You owe your neighbor one thousand dollars. You are paralyzed, completely unable to make money in order to pay your debt. In spite of your paralysis you must pay. Your neighbor has a rightful claim to the one thousand dollars, and he brings you to court. Appearing before the judge you are ready to be sentenced. Then a friend comes and gives your neighbor one thousand dollars. The friend explains that this one thousand dollars is to be reckoned as your payment. Seeing your friend's action the judge declares you free from the debt. The judge reckons the money of your friend to be your money. You leave the court room in terms of peace with your neighbor.

God is the Judge. You are the sinner loaded with debt. Christ Jesus is your friend. His life and His work are freely given to you. God, the Judge, reckons Christ's work to be yours. He declares you free from all debt. This is the picture of justification. You are "justified by his grace as a gift, through the redemption which is in Christ Jesus" (Rom. 3:24). You are right with God, and you can live together with God on terms of peace and love.

We sinners get right with God by faith. We cannot work our way into God's love. Nothing we do can make us right with God. Not even our best actions such as worship, prayer, Bible reading, or love to God and our fellowman can help us get right with God. All our actions, even the best we can bring, are still imperfect and stained with sin. "For we hold that a man is justified by faith apart from works of law" (Rom. 3:28). ". . . Yet who know that a man is not justified by works of the law but through faith in Jesus Christ, even we have believed in Christ Jesus, in order to be justified by faith in Christ, and not by works of the law, because by works of the law shall no one be justified" (Gal. 2:16).

The Consecrated Life

Peace with God means service for God. The sinner freed from his debts uses his freedom to honor the God who made him free. The sinner is saved to serve. "You are not your own; you were bought with a price. So glorify God in your body" (I Cor. 6:20). Your life surrendered to Jesus for salvation is also surrendered for service.

The consecrated life is a God-centered life. The whole purpose of the Christian life is to glorify God and enjoy Him forever. Everything the Christian does must center on God—the Father, and the Son, and the Holy Spirit—"So whether you eat or drink, or whatever you do, do all to the glory of God" (I Cor. 10:31). Christ gives Christians a new place in this world. "But you are a chosen race, a royal priesthood, a holy nation, God's own people, that you may declare the wonderful deeds of him who called you out of darkness into his marvelous light" (I Peter 2:9).

1. ____________ is the act of God whereby He declares the sinner free because the work of the Savior has become the work of the guilty, but now believing sinner.
2. A sinner is saved to ____________.

LESSON 7

The New Life in Fellowship

A citizen is part of his nation. A soldier is a member of the army. So a Christian belongs to the church. A citizen cannot be a citizen without belonging to the nation. The soldier cannot be a soldier without being in the army. So, a Christian cannot be a Christian without belonging to the church.

The Church

The church of Jesus Christ is a band of believing sinners who rely on their Savior for salvation. The church is the gathering "of true Christian believers, all expecting their salvation in Jesus Christ, being washed by his blood, sanctified and sealed by the Holy Spirit" (Belgic Confession, Article XXVII). The Christian believer becomes a spiritual brother of every other Christian believer, and together they have a common life. "There is one body and one Spirit . . . one Lord, one faith, one baptism, one God and Father of us all, who is above all and through all and in all" (Eph. 4:4-6).

The Bible uses many names to describe this band of saved sinners. The church is called the *Body of Christ*, the *Bride of Christ*, the *Household of Faith*, the *Sheep of the Great Shepherd*, and the *Temple of God*. Each name describes some special quality of the church. The important thing to remember is this: It is Christ Jesus who makes the church what it is. His life gives heart to the church. His truth is the message of the church. His Word is the standard by which the church measures its action. His work is the hope of the church.

1. The __________ of Jesus Christ is a band of believing Christians who rely on their Savior for salvation.

The Church and the Churches

This one church is seen by man as many churches. There are Christian Reformed, Lutheran, Baptist, Methodist, Presbyterian churches, and many others. These churches are called denominations, and each denomination has its special way of working. Some of these churches really try to be obedient to Christ's will as made known in the Bible. Other denominations believe and practice only that which makes sense to them, using the rule of human reason as the standard for their actions.

The newly-born Christian is often confused when he sees all these churches. His confusion grows worse when he hears each of these churches claiming to be the true church. When this happens the new Christian must do one important thing. He must take the official teaching and public actions of the denominations in his neighborhood and measure them by the truth of the Bible. The Christian must work and pray in order to follow after Christ's will as made known in the Bible.

This is not always done. Some Christians act carelessly. They do not seem to care which of the denominations they join. In mistaken sincerity they say, "It makes little difference which church I join. The important thing is to love Jesus as my Savior." Such thinking forgets that loving Jesus includes loving the Word of their Savior. Anyone who genuinely loves the Lord will desire to remain loyal to all of Christ's truths. Therefore the Christian must join a denomination which officially teaches the whole Word of God and which publicly practices this truth. This means prayerful study on our part and loyal service in the church which the Christian joins. There are three important factors to be considered: 1. The preaching of the gospel must be loyal to the whole Bible. The churches today must follow Paul's example in the church of Ephesus: "For I did not shrink from declaring to you the whole counsel of God" (Acts 20:27). No church should ride its pet teachings and neglect other truths. The practice in the Christian Reformed Church of preaching according to the plan of the Heidelberg Catechism helps to bring the full range of Biblical truth. 2. The sacraments of Holy Baptism and the Holy Supper must be observed according to the regulations of Christ. Here too private ideas must bow to the Word of the Lord. 3. Christian supervision must be carried on loyally and lovingly. This is called Christian discipline. This work is carried on by the whole membership (Matt. 18:15ff) and especially by the ruling officers of the church (Matt. 16:19). Christians care for each other and demonstrate this in fellowship. These three factors are called the marks of the true church. The Christian who prayerfully and intelligently watches for these three marks will join a Christ-honoring denomination.

1. A Christian can determine which denomination teaches the whole Word of __________ and publicly __________ this truth by using the following criteria:
   a. Is the __________ loyal to the whole Bible?
   b. Are the __________ observed according to the regulations of Christ?
   c. Is the work of Christian __________ carried on by the whole membership?

The Word

The Christian must live as did the Berean Christians in the land of Greece. "Now these Jews were more noble than those in Thessalonica, for they received the word with all eagerness, examining the scriptures daily to see if these things were so" (Acts 17:11). The Word of God was the food of their lives. Peter urged his readers, "Like newborn babes, long for the pure spiritual milk, that by it you may grow up to salvation" (I Peter 2:2).

This includes faithful attendance of the public worship services in your church. Through the preaching of the gospel, Christ works wonders of salvation and strength in the lives of His disciples. It also includes private devotions for the Christian. He must take time to listen to God as He speaks in and through the Bible. Only as this Word of God enters into the Christian life will there be strength, joy, comfort, wisdom, and other blessings. This includes also taking time for family worship. Often this is done at meal times where the Bible is read in the presence of the whole family. Christ Jesus has promised to use the Word of truth as a means of genuine spiritual growth.

1. Receiving the Word includes faithful attendance of worship __________ and private __________.

The Sacrament of Baptism

Christ has given two sacraments to His church. These are baptism and the Lord's Supper. These are the New Testament counterparts of circumcision and the Passover which were practiced by Israel in the Old Testament age.

Baptism is an outward sign of an inward blessing. In picture language it tells us what happens in the soul of one who believes in Jesus Christ. The outward sign is water. Water is used for cleansing. When a minister of the gospel sprinkles water on the forehead of a believer, this pictures the inward washing of the soul by the blood of Jesus Christ. Baptism also tells us something about our union with Jesus Christ and with God. A person is baptized *into* the name of God—the Father, and the Son, and the Holy Spirit. The word *into* underlines the truth that a believing sinner who is baptized is joined to God. Paul speaks this way in Romans 6:3: We are "baptized into Christ Jesus." Being joined to God in Christ we are cleansed from all defilement of sin.

Baptism is also a seal. A seal confirms and establishes what is pictured in the symbol. A seal on a diploma confirms the truth of the words written on it. Baptism is a seal used by Christ to confirm and establish in our lives the blessings of His salvation. In the Old Testament, Abraham received circumcision as a "sign or seal of the righteousness which he had by faith while he was still uncircumcised" (Rom. 4:11). Baptism in the New Testament takes the place of circumcision (Col. 2:11, 12).

Therefore, we know that baptism is a seal of God upon His promises of salvation.

In the ceremony of baptism there are three factors which we see and one factor which we do not see. We see the minister sprinkling the water, the water being used, and the person being baptized. However, we do not see the working of the Holy Spirit. It is the Holy Spirit who works in the sacrament according to Christ's promise. He works to impart the blessings of salvation. The power of baptism does not rest in the minister, nor in the water, nor in the believer who is baptized. The power of baptism rests in the Holy Spirit. He uses this ceremony to declare and seal the blessings of salvation unto believers.

1. Baptism which has taken the place of the Old Testament ____________ is a ____________ and ____________ of the promises of salvation.
2. Although invisible, the ____________ works in baptism to impart the blessings of the sacrament to the believer.

Infant Baptism

Children of believing parents must be baptized. At this point we differ from the Baptist churches. There are good reasons why we believe in the practice of baptizing the infants of believers. It is clear that children of Old Testament believers received the sign and seal of circumcision. They were included in God's covenant of grace. If children were to be excluded from God's covenant of grace in the New Testament, we would expect God to make this plain. But God does not command children to be excluded. The opposite is true: "For the promise is to you and to your children . . ." (Acts 2:39). God's covenant of grace is essentially the same in both the Old and the New Testaments.

Baptism in the New Testament has the same meaning as circumcision in the Old Testament. Baptism takes the place of circumcision in the Old Testament. "In him also you were circumcised with a circumcision made without hands, by putting off the body of flesh in the circumcision of Christ; and you were buried with him in baptism, in which you were also raised with him through faith in the working of God, who raised him from the dead" (Col. 2:11, 12). Because baptism takes the place of circumcision we dare not exclude children from this sign and seal. Lydia, the first European convert, and the Philippian jailor were baptized by Paul together with their families (Acts 16:15, 33). The blessings pictured and sealed in baptism belong to believers and their children, not to adult believers alone.

1. As children were included in The Old Testament covenant of grace and were circumcised, so in The New Testament children of believers must be ___________.

The Lord's Supper

The Lord's Supper is also called Holy Communion. It is the second New Testament sacrament. It was instituted by Jesus while He celebrated His last Passover feast with His disciples.

The Lord's Supper is a sign. It is the gospel in picture form. The broken bread signifies Christ's broken body. The poured-out wine represents His shed blood. Jesus tells us why His body was broken and His blood shed. "For this is my blood of the covenant, which is poured out for many for the forgiveness of sins" (Matt. 26:28). As believers look at the bread and wine of the Lord's Supper, they see in picture form the fact of Christ dying on the cross for their sins.

By means of this Holy Supper the Lord gives strength. Just as the ordinary foods we eat give strength to our bodies, so the elements of the bread and the wine are used by the Holy Spirit to make our faith and Christian life strong. In a strange and wonderful way believers are joined to the body and blood of Jesus by the working of the Holy Spirit. Just how this happens we do not know, but that it does happen can be experienced at the table of the Lord.

The Lord's Supper is a badge of the Christian profession. By taking the bread and the wine the Christian proclaims the

Lord's death until He comes (I Cor. 11:26). At the Lord's Supper believers raise a memorial to the death of Christ which is their source of life.

The Lord's Supper is also a fellowship with other Christians. As many berries pressed together produce one wine, so believers are more and more joined together in the blessed fellowship of the saved. As sinners taste the love of Christ in their lives, they radiate love to each other in the richest and sweetest companionship found in this world.

Great blessings are given by Christ at His table. This high privilege is not given to just any and everyone. A person must examine himself. Paul says, "Whoever, therefore, eats the bread or drinks the cup of the Lord in an unworthy manner will be guilty of profaning the body and blood of the Lord. Let a man examine himself, and so eat of the bread and drink of the cup" (I Cor. 11:27, 28). This self-examination revolves around three things: First, a person must personally know himself to be a sinner in the sight of God. Second, he must genuinely believe he is saved by the Lord Jesus. Third, he must promise to live a godly and obedient life. The saved sinner comes to the Lord's Supper in repentance, faith, and obedience. Such sinners are blessed by the Lord who uses this means to feed the new life of the Christian.

1. The Lord's Supper makes our __________ strong and we remember the ____________ of Christ, and join together in the fellowship of the saved.
2. Only those who know themselves to be __________, believe themselves to be __________ and promise to live a godly __________ may partake of the Lord's Supper.

Prayer

Genuine prayer is like a great highway with traffic going both ways. In this holy mystery of prayer man draws close to God and God comes nigh to man. As this holy and intimate fellowship is experienced, the Christian enters into one of the supreme delights of his new-born life.

The praying Christian follows the example of his Savior. Jesus often communed with His Father in prayer. At times He would rise before dawn and pray (Mark 1:35). Other times He would spend the whole night in prayer (Luke 6:12). During moments of great stress such as He endured in the garden of Gethsemane Jesus entered the holy sanctuary of prayer (Luke 22:41). From these hallowed moments of prayer our substitute drew strength to carry out the Father's will for our salvation.

The longer the disciples followed after Jesus, the more they realized the importance of prayer in their lives. One day while they watched the Savior pray, they asked Jesus to teach them the perfect prayer which we now know as The Lord's Prayer. The more thoroughly we understand the meaning of this prayer, the better we will be able to pray.

Jesus sets the proper mood for prayer in the address, "Our Father who art in heaven." Because Jesus has forgiven our sins we may talk with God as Father. He loves us, provides for us, and directs our lives with infinite wisdom and tender compassion. Because God is the Christian's Father, the Christian enters into a delightful and close fellowship with God. We must, however, catch the meaning of the place where the Father lives. God dwells in the resplendent glory of heaven. There He is surrounded by millions of worshiping angels. The words "in heaven" emphasize the need for reverence, awe, worship, and adoration in our prayers.

After addressing God in the mood of love and reverence, Jesus outlines the things we ask for in our prayers. Notice that God Himself forms the first focus of our petitions. The whole life of Christ is God-centered. Jesus tells us to pray in this manner, "Hallowed be Thy name, Thy Kingdom come, Thy will be done, On earth as it is in heaven" (Matt. 6:9, 10). It is God's honor, His glory, and His Kingdom which becomes the basic concern of the true Christian.

Such prayer involves many practical things for our daily lives. We ask God to order our lives in such a way that His wonderful name be praised on our account. In this prayer we beg the Lord to rule over our lives by His Word and Spirit. To take the Lord's prayer upon our lips is to ask our Father to have His own way in our lives. Every Christian knows how hard it is to renounce our own wills and surrender everything to God. In our prayer life we practice the truth that we are no longer our own but that we belong to our faithful Savior, Jesus Christ. As we sincerely make this prayer the expression of our lives we discover that our new life grows more and more Christ-like.

But there is still more involved in true prayer. Jesus also taught His disciples to pray for their needs. This is heard in the words, "Give us this day our daily bread, And forgive us our debts, As we also have forgiven our debtors; And lead us not into temptation, But deliver us from evil" (Matt. 6:11-13). Included in these few words are all the basic needs for man's body and his soul. The Savior is interested in our bodies, the clothes we wear, the food we eat, the health we enjoy. Freely, as a child coming to his parents, we may go to our Father and ask Him for these things that we need. The Savior is also interested in our peace of soul, in a conscience freed from the burden of guilt. He urges us to take these needs to our Father who is in heaven. And since no Christian is a Christian by himself, but always in fellowship with others, the Lord reminds us about our debt to love and forgive those with whom we live. The interpersonal relationships of life are also included in the prayers of true believers.

So we see the Savior teaching us to take all our needs to our blessed Father. As we travel the road to heaven in prayer, God Himself returns and crowns our lives with His gifts of grace.

Satan, the enemy supreme, works hard in the sanctuary of prayer. He tries to worm his way into our prayer life, thus destroying its delights. In the Bible we discover some of the reasons why prayer often loses its power and its pleasure in the Christian's life. Secret sins (Ps. 66:18), indifference (Prov. 1:28), the neglect of mercy (Prov. 21:13), stubbornness (Zech. 7:13), instability (James 1: 6, 7), and self-indulgence (James 4:3) are some of the insidious barriers, erected by the enemy, which block the road of prayer. The Christian must continue to examine his own heart lest he merely repeat some words and fail to pray. Even in the holy sanctuary of prayer there is need for daily repentance as well as faith.

Any Christian who expects his new life to grow must pray. Jesus put it plainly when He said, "They ought always to pray and not lose heart" (Luke 18:1). The person who perseveres in prayer discovers many new and rich experiences of spiritual power. Christ gave us this beautiful promise to encourage us in our prayer life: "And whatever you ask in prayer, you will receive, if you have faith" (Matt. 21:22). In moments when our prayers seem so futile and in seasons when Christ gives us different things than we ask for, let us hold fast His Word in faith. Here too the persistent Christian is the victorious Christian.

The Christain should organize his daily routine of life in such a way that he never neglects his prayers. We must find moments when we can be alone with our God in our inner chambers. We must take time at family meals to achieve the beauty of a praying family. In our church life there ought to be seasons of common prayer as the members of the church link heart with heart in the holy moments of praise and prayer. A praying Christian is a God-glorifying Christian. "Let us then with confidence draw near to the throne of grace, that we may receive mercy and find grace to help in time of need" (Heb. 4:16).

1. In the mystery of prayer, __________ and __________ draw close together.
2. The address, "Our Father who art in heaven" tells us __________ must be addressed in __________ and reverence.
3. "Hallowed be thy name, Thy kingdom come and Thy will be done" tells us that the Christian's chief concern in life is God and His __________.
4. Jesus taught that we also must pray for our __________ such as food, health, freedom from guilt, peace of mind.
5. Since prayer is essential for the growth of the new life, __________ works insidiously to destroy prayer life. Therefore the Christian's life should be so organized that he participates in private, family, and church __________.

LESSON 8

New Obedience

In what ways should the Christian serve God? How can a saved person know that his actions and attitudes honor the Lord? It may happen that someone thinks he is honoring God while in fact he is dishonoring Him. We need a reliable standard by which to measure life's actions and attitudes. This standard is provided by God. The whole Bible is the only rule by which we measure our obedience, and the Ten Commandments found in Exodus 20 give us a summary of God's will for our new lives as we grow in joyful thanksgiving.

Special Obedience

The Christian's obedience is a special kind of obedience. It is the obedience of a new creature, of a saved person. It is obedience which arises out of thankfulness for salvation received. It is a joyful obedience given by one who has tasted the love of God.

This fact becomes plain as you read the introduction to the Ten Commandments. "I am the Lord your God, who brought you out of the land of Egypt, out of the house of bondage" (Exod. 20:2). Egypt was the country which had enslaved the Israelites. God freed His people from this slavery. Because God had delivered His people, they were to obey the law. Their obedience was a proof of their gratitude. This story of liberation from Egypt is an Old Testament fact which tells basically the same story as the liberation from sin through Jesus Christ. The proof of the Christian's gratitude is the joyful obedience he gives to God's law.

The fact that the Christian's obedience is a new obedience is an important fact. A person who tries to obey God's law in order to become saved is dishonoring the Lord Jesus. There is nothing more dishonoring to Christ than to act as if His work were unnecessary or insufficient for our salvation. This is done if a person tries to obey the law in order to achieve salvation. Besides this, such a person will always live in fear and uncertainty. He will never know whether his obedience is good enough and acceptable to God. Therefore we must remember this: A sinner may not obey in order to become saved, but must obey just because he is saved through Jesus Christ. Salvation makes obedience new with the newness of gratitude, love, and joy.

1. A Christian shows gratitude for deliverance from the bondage of sin by joyful ____________ to God's law.
2. Obedience to God's law to ____________ salvation is acting as though Christ's work were not sufficient.

Commandment One

"You shall have no other gods before me" (Exod. 20:3).

The Ten Commandments begin with God because God is always first in the Christian life. God wants us to acknowledge Him *alone*. Life's love, hope, honor, and praise belong to God. The Christian must worship God *alone*, with a full life from a full heart.

There is more idolatry in life than we realize. Man has many gods. Anyone or anything that we love more than God is really a false god. Sometimes we value things more than God. There are many such gods. Self, friends, family, success, the social club, money, become gods for many. These things and values may be good in themselves, but they must be kept out of first place. First place belongs to God. The writer of Psalm 73:25 caught the meaning of this commandment: "Whom have I in heaven but thee? And there is nothing upon earth that I desire besides thee."

Commandment Two

"You shall not make for yourself a graven image . . . you shall now bow down to them or serve them . . ." (Exod. 20:4, 5).

Besides commanding us to worship Him alone, God demands that we worship Him in the right way. The way of worship is referred to in the second commandment. To glorify God we must worship Him in the way which He has commanded in His Word. We must not try to improve on God's instructions.

The second commandment can be disobeyed in many different ways. God's Old Testament people tried to improve their worship by building a golden calf at Mt. Sinai (Exod. 32). Later, King Jeroboam (I Kings 12) set up his altars and images at Bethel and Dan. Some people try to improve on God's directions for true worship by making crucifixes, altars, and statues of various kinds. Others, and this is much more clever, make mental pictures of God which are contrary to the truth of God's Word. For example, they think of God as a good-hearted person who does not take sin too seriously. Or they think they can ignore the services of Christ's church on Sunday and worship God just as well at a good trout stream.

"God is spirit, and those who worship him must worship in spirit and truth" (John 4:24). The Spirit leads us to Jesus Christ who is the Truth. He is the only Mediator between God and the sinner. The Christian must worship God through Jesus Christ and in submission to the Word of God.

Commandment Three

"You shall not take the name of the Lord your God in vain . . ." (Exod. 20:7).

A name is important because it identifies you as you associate with other people. By means of your name you are kept distinct from others and you exercise fellowship with others. A good name opens up new opportunities, and you want it to be treated with respect.

God's name is His revelation through which He comes into fellowship with His creatures. A flower, a ray of sunshine, a star is part of God's name. "How majestic is thy name in all the earth!" (Ps. 8:1). After sin blinded our eyes, God made Himself known by using other names. The "God of Abraham," the "I am that I am," the "Father of mercy" are a few of these names. God's most beautiful name is read in Jesus Christ.

All these names of God must be treated with reverence, respect, awe, and adoration. The third commandment demands that we use the holy names of God in fear and reverence. In worshipful awe and cautious reverence we truly confess and glorify God.

There are many ways in which the name of God is abused. Swearing and cursing are obvious violations of this third commandment. So is perjury—the sin of lying while under oath. Preachers can disobey this commandment when they use God's name in preaching for such selfish reasons as gaining popularity and applause. The worshiping congregation can dishonor God's name in a church service when they carelessly allow their minds to wander. When we fail to use God's name in certain circumstances we win against this third word of the law. Remember this: If your name is important to you, how much more important is the name of Him who made and saved you.

Commandment Four

"Remember the sabbath day to keep it holy" (Exod. 20:8).

The Sabbath is a special day. It was first observed in the garden of Eden. "So God blessed the seventh day, and hallowed it . . ." (Gen. 2:3). This special day was given to man for two reasons. First, God invited man to enjoy the works of God in special companionship with God. God wanted man to share in that pleasure which God Himself enjoyed when He completed the work of creating the world. Second, God wanted man to have some free time. God made man to work in God's world. God made man to be master of creation in God's name and for God's sake. But God did not want man to work all the time. He also wanted him to rest. If you understand these two reasons you will understand the words of Jesus, "The sabbath was made for man, not man for the sabbath" (Mark 2:27).

The Sabbath is now observed on the first day of the week. Jesus Christ and His apostles substituted the first day for the seventh day. It is the Lord's Day. On this day we must use our time for the purposes which God set aside this day. It is to be a day of spiritual refreshment, physical rest, and Christian service. On this day we receive spiritual blessings from our Savior. On this day we enjoy some physical rest. On this day we enjoy performing special spiritual services for which we have so little time during the week. It is a day in which we delight to worship God in the company of the saved. It is a day in which we go about visiting the sick, the lonely, and the needy.

This commandment is widely disobeyed. In countless ways people use this day for themselves, apart from God's companionship. A sure sign of little love for the Lord is the way in which people abuse the Lord's day. In order to discover what you should do and should not do on this day, ask yourself this question: Am I using the Lord's Day for the purposes the Lord intended? As you use this day in God's way, you will discover seasons of joy and refreshment in your life.

Christ's Summary

The first four commandments focus on our duties toward God. Jesus gave this summary: "You shall love the Lord your God with all your heart, and with all your soul, and with all your mind. This is the great and first commandment" (Matt. 22:37, 38). The Christian's new obedience is loving God above all. This love is our answer to God's love for us in Christ Jesus our Lord.

Commandment Five

"Honor your father and your mother . . ." (Exod. 20:12).

The fifth word is a bridge between the two parts of God's law. In the first table of the law we discover our responsibilities to God. The second table concerns our responsibilities to our fellowmen. We must honor, respect, and obey the authority of parents because they take the place of God in our young lives. God is pleased to rule our lives through them. In this sense the fifth word concerns our duty to God. But it is also true that this commandment tells about all delegated authority such as is found in the state, in the church, and other social institutions. Here we come close to our duties involving our fellowmen. For this reason we can speak of this commandment as a bridge joining the two tables of God's law.

In the home children learn how to live with fellow human beings. It is the duty of parents to train their children in the fear of God. As parents bring God's will to bear upon the lives of their children, sons and daughters learn respect, honor, and obedience. If children do not learn to follow the regulations of God in the home, they will be unable to follow the regulations of life. And if parents ignore, abuse, or ill-train their children, they contribute to the breakdown of society.

Commandment Six

"You shall not kill" (Exod. 20:13).

God wants His child to love life. Obviously, murder is wrong. But this commandment covers much more. It forbids anything that is harmful to the physical well-being of ourselves and others. Jesus said, "But I say to you that every one who is angry with his brother shall be liable to judgment . . ." (Matt. 5:22). John caught Jesus' meaning and wrote, "Any one who hates his brother is a murderer" (I John 3:15). Loss of temper joined with insulting words is murder. If looks could kill, many people would be dead. The desire for revenge is murder. God demands that we seek the welfare of our fellowmen.

This means paying attention to the proper regulations for health. This means watching how one drives his car. This means listening to all those precautions which are given to help safeguard our lives. The Christian will learn to love his own life for God's sake and love his neighbor as himself.

Commandment Seven

"You shall not commit adultery" (Exod. 20:14).

God has ordained that there be one husband and one wife in the home which is the basic unit of society. Marriage is an unbreakable bond. "What therefore God has joined together, let no man put asunder" (Matt. 19:6). Within the sacred bond of marriage sex drives are to be satisfied. To satisfy sex desires in other ways than within marriage is forbidden.

Here again, God's will has wide application. This commandment includes strict morality all along the line. Jesus gave the depth dimension to this seventh commandment when He said, "Everyone who looks at a woman lustfully has already committed adultery with her in his heart" (Matt. 5:28). To entertain murderous thoughts in one's heart is to commit murder, and to entertain adulterous thoughts in the heart is to commit adultery. In a sexually permissive time this word needs new emphasis and understanding.

Commandment Eight

"You shall not steal" (Exod. 20:15).

God owns all things. "The earth is the Lord's and the fulness thereof . . ." (Ps. 24:1). The divine owner has given certain property rights to man. God has given the earth to the children of men. We must use this world and its gifts for God's praise and the welfare of our fellow men. We may never gain our wealth at the expense of someone else. God gave man rights of possession so that his material goods might be used in spiritual service. The Christian must respect these God-given property rights of others.

This commandment also covers a broad area. Tax evasion is stealing. To overwork and underpay employees is robbery. Refusing to do a good day's work for a fair wage is stealing. The Christian does not expect to get something for nothing. This eighth word of the law requires diligent work, conserving and consolidating our gains in thrift and economy. It also includes using our gifts for the welfare of our neighbors. Paul urged the thief to stop stealing. He had to start working and then use his gains to help those in need (Eph. 4:28). God turns burglars into benefactors.

Commandment Nine

"You shall not bear false witness against your neighbor" (Exod. 20:16).

Loving our neighbor means respecting his rights. To disobey God's Word as described in the second table of the law is to rob a man of the things most precious to him: his life (killing), his home and honor (adultery), his property (stealing), and also his good name. A good name is to be desired above great riches.

This commandment covers a great deal of ground. It includes the law courts and the sin of perjury. It also includes idle gossip, deliberate exaggeration and distortion of the truth, and all slander. We can break this commandment by listening to unkind rumors and then passing these rumors on to others.

God is the God of truth. He requires that His children always speak the truth, in love. Satan is the great deceiver, the liar from the beginning. The lie is one of the chief weapons in his war against the kingdom of Jesus Christ. He started his lying campaign in the garden of Eden and continues it today. He delights to condemn the godly and to condone the godless. The Christian must love the truth and hate the lie in every form. Then he honors the God of truth.

Commandment Ten

"You shall not covet your neighbor's house . . . or anything that is your neighbor's" (Exod. 20:17).

God's law is very broad. It begins with God and ends deep in the heart of man. This commandment defines our duty in terms of the inner desires of the soul. It covers the area of life where the laws of the state cannot reach. The police and courts of the land are not concerned with making rules to govern what a person desires. God, however, is concerned about it.

The Christian must not become jealous or envious of what someone else possesses. He is to rejoice in the prosperity and blessings of his neighbor. The Christian does not put a premium on the material things of life. "Take heed," said Jesus, "and beware of all covetousness; for a man's life does not consist in the abundance of his possessions" (Luke 12:15). "For what does it profit a man, to gain the whole world and forfeit his life?" (Mark 8:36). The Christian seeks first the kingdom of God and his righteousness. "Covetousness is idolatry," wrote Paul (Col. 3:5), but "there is great gain in godliness with contentment" (I Tim. 6:6). The Christian watches the desires of the heart, for out of the heart are the issues of life (Prov. 4:23).

Reacting to God's Law

The more seriously the Christian tries to live according to all the commandments of the law, the more he sees his own sinfulness and ugliness. God's law exposes the sinner's life. ". . .Through the law comes knowledge of sin" (Rom. 3:20). Under the conviction of his sin the believer cries out with Paul, "Wretched man that I am! Who will deliver me from this body of death? Thanks be to God through Jesus Christ our Lord!" (Rom. 7:24, 25). The Christian begins to understand more clearly the words of John, "If we say we have no sin, we deceive ourselves . . . If we say we have not sinned we make him [God] a liar, and his word is not in us" (I John 1:8, 10). The sinner continually turns to God for mercy and tastes the goodness of God's forgiving love in Jesus Christ.

The Christian also tries hard to grow in true obedience. Grateful for salvation, rejoicing in forgiveness, the believer seeks to glorify God by obeying His law. Looking to his Savior, the new-born sinner says, "I can do all things in him who strengthens me" (Phil. 4:13).

1. As the sinner tries to obey God's __________ his life is increasingly exposed as sinful and ugly.
2. The __________ however, continues to work to glorify God by obeying His law.

LESSON 1

Study Aids

What I Confess

1. The basis for my confession of Jesus Christ is the inspired Word of God.
2. The whole Bible is inspired. This means that the Holy Spirit moved men to write the Scriptures and guided them in their work so that they wrote the Word of God without error.
3. All sixty-six books of the inspired Bible are infallible and worthy of shaping my beliefs and patterning my conduct. The whole Bible and only the Bible is the standard for my life.
4. I thank God for giving me the testimony of the Holy Spirit which enables me to accept the Bible's claim to be the Word of God.
5. The testimony of the Holy Spirit is God's special work in my heart which opens my eyes, ears, and heart to the presence of His truth in the Bible. Without this work I would still be blind to the truth of God.
6. As I continue reading and reflecting on God's Word I prayerfully ask the Holy Spirit to lead me into the riches of divine truth.
7. I believe that God created everything good in the beginning. God created everything according to His plan and for His praise.

Review Questions and Answers

1. *What does the doctrine of the Trinity mean for the Christian?*
   The Christian confesses that one God lives as three persons—Father, Son, and Holy Spirit.

2. *What is the Bible?*
   The Bible is the inspired and infallible Word of God consisting of sixty-six books.

3. *What do you understand by the doctrine of inspiration?*
   This doctrine teaches that the Holy Spirit guided the human authors of the Bible to write down God's Word without error.

4. *Why do many people refuse to acknowledge the Bible as God's Word?*
   Such people have not asked for nor received the gift of the testimony of the Holy Spirit.

5. *What is the testimony of the Holy Spirit?*
   It is a special work of the Holy Spirit by which the sinner's mind is convinced of the truth of the Bible's message.

Digging Deeper

1. How did we get so many translations of the Bible? Which is the best one?
2. Why do Protestants not include the books of the Apocrypha in the Bible?
3. Why is it so imperative to confess the truth of inspiration?
4. What do those who do not believe the teaching of inspiration say about the Bible?
5. What do Articles III through VII of the *Belgic Confession* teach about the Bible?
6. What is the difference between saying, "The Bible *is* God's Word" and "The Bible *contains* God's Word"?

LESSON 2

What I Confess

1. There are many questions about the origin of the world which the Bible does not answer. I do not know just how God made everything, nor do I know just when God created the world. But I know that the record of Genesis 1 and 2 is historically correct. It is a record of what God actually did at the beginning of this world.
2. The facts discovered by scientists of various kinds do not contradict the truths contained in the Bible. This does not mean that I know all about science or the Bible. But I do know this: God's revelation in the Bible and God's revelation in nature and history never contradict each other. My God and Father is a God of truth whenever and wherever He speaks.
3. As a creature I was made in God's image and likeness. I was made to reflect God on a creaturely level. I was blessed with a perfect nature. But in my sin I lost these unique gifts. I can now only be the full image of God in Jesus Christ my Lord.
4. In Paradise God made with my first parents an arrangement called a covenant. God willed man to enjoy a life of blessed fellowship with Him in the way of obedient faith. I confess that I fell in Adam and can only be received back into God's loving friendship in Jesus Christ.
5. I believe that God works to take care of His whole creation. This

activity of God is called His providence. It includes the act of preserving the world and the act of governing all things unto the praise of the glory of His grace.

6. God never works by chance. He fashioned a plan from before the foundations of the world. In sovereignty, wisdom, love, and righteousness God works everything out according to the counsels of His will.
7. God's plan for sinful man includes the election unto salvation of some sinners in Jesus Christ. These sinners are no better than any others who are passed by. God chose them just because He loved them in Christ. I believe I am one of those whom God has elected in Christ. God and his free grace are the determining fact in my life as a saved sinner.
8. Even though I cannot figure out God's ways with His world, I shall humbly follow the teachings of His Word. As a saved sinner I shall declare the glorious gospel of salvation so that others may come to know this wonderful God and His salvation. Rather than arguing with God when I cannot understand His ways, I shall continue to pray for grace that I may adore and serve Him all the days of my life.
9. In trying to answer the objections raised to the Christian faith I shall try to discover answers contained in the Bible. In my intellectual struggles I shall work and pray so that every thought may be brought into the captivity of Jesus Christ my Savior and Lord.

Review Questions and Answers

1. *What does the Bible teach as to the origin of man and this world?*
   God created man and this world by an act of His will.
2. *Do the Bible and the facts discovered by modern scientists contradict each other?*
   There is no real contradiction between the Bible and scientific facts because God's truth of general revelation does not contradict God's truth of special revelation.
3. *How did God create man?*
   God created man "good" and in the image of God.
4. *How did the first man Adam live in the presence of God?*
   Adam lived with God in an arrangement called a covenant on terms of obedience and friendship.
5. *How did Adam break this covenant?*
   Adam disobeyed God's will by eating of the forbidden fruit.
6. *What is divine providence?*
   This is an act of God whereby He preserves all things and governs everything according to His plan.

7. *What is divine predestination?*
   It is the act of God which involves the unconditional election of some men to be saved in Christ and the passing by and righteous condemnation of others.

8. *How can a sinner know that he is one of God's elect?*
   The sinner who truly believes in the Lord Jesus Christ is an elect person because God elected sinners in Jesus Christ.

9. *Does God truly offer salvation to all sinners who hear the gospel?*
   God graciously offers salvation to all in the way of repentance and faith.

Digging Deeper

1. What do various Bible students mean when they call the creation story of Genesis a myth?
2. How old is the human race? The present universe?
3. What is meant by the phrases, "the image of God in the narrower sense" and "the image of God in the broader sense"?
4. In what ways can the Christian read too much into the Bible?
5. What does Romans 5:12 ff. teach us about Adam's unique position in Paradise?
6. What do the *Heidelberg Catechism*, Articles XII and XIV, teach about creation?
7. What is the relationship of such scientific laws as the law of gravitation to God's preserving activity?
8. What is the difference between the Arminian and the Reformed view of God's counsel?
9. How do Hezekiah's prayer (II Kings 20), Daniel's prayer (Dan. 9), and Nehemiah's prayer (Neh. 1) fit in with the doctrine of God's providence and plan?
10. What is meant by the will of God's decree and the will of God's command?
11. What is the practical significance of the doctrine of divine providence? See *Heidelberg Catechism*, Questions 27 and 28, and the *Belgic Confession*, Article 13.
12. What do the *Canons of Dort* teach about election and reprobation?

LESSON 3

What I Confess

1. God's enemy, the devil, is also my enemy. I realize that he wants to destroy my life by leading me away from the truth and love of God.

2. The sin of Adam and Eve in Paradise was rebellion against God. They should have obeyed God's Word just because it was God's Word. I do not, however, want to excuse myself from their sin. I am also guilty in the sight of God and justly deserve His anger.
3. The punishment of God against sin is terrible. It involves three kinds of death. There is spiritual, physical, and eternal death. Without Jesus as my Savior I would have to endure this death. I rejoice in the free gift of eternal life in Jesus Christ, my Lord.
4. There are two facts involved in my sin. First, there is my own corrupt nature. This sinful nature involves me in all kinds of separate sinful actions such as greed, pride, unbelief, and many others. Second, there is my guilt. This means that I am worthy of the just punishments of God. The more I understand about my sin, the more I hate it.
5. I was born as a person totally depraved. This means that I was unable to do anything thoroughly pleasing to my God. It also means that I did not want to honor and please my God. Only Jesus Christ can give me a new nature by sending the Holy Spirit into my life. As a saved sinner I can say, "Once I was dead but now I live."

Review Questions and Answers

1. *How did Satan tempt our first parents in the garden of Eden?*
   Satan twisted God's Word, sowed the seeds of doubt in man's heart, and urged man to disobey God's commandment.
2. *What is the basic characteristic of sin?*
   Sin is proud, self-centered disobedience of God's will.
3. *How does God punish sin?*
   God provides the unrepentant sinner with spiritual, physical, and eternal death.
4. *In what ways does the first sin of Adam concern us?*
   In two ways: 1. He is our father according to the flesh. 2. He is the head of the covenant of works.
5. *What is the doctrine of total depravity?*
   This is the Biblical teaching that tells us that the unsaved sinner is sinful in every part of his personality and has an inborn tendency toward sin.

Digging Deeper

1. How is Satan described in I Peter 5:8 and II Corinthians 11:14?
2. What does Article XV of the *Belgic Confession* teach about original sin?
3. What special punishments did God assign to man and woman in

Genesis 3:16ff?

4. What do the *Canons of Dort* teach in the Second and Third Heads of Doctrine about man's ability to save himself?
5. Which group of people today deny the reality of the place called hell?

LESSON 4

What I Confess

1. Jesus Christ is my Savior. He served as a substitute for me. I believe on Him as a perfect Savior, perfectly suited to fill the needs of my sinful life.
2. I rejoice in a *human* Savior. As a human being I have sinned. Jesus was completely human. He knows my special needs and has answered these needs in every way.
3. My Savior is the Son of God. If Jesus were not God, I could never be saved. Only God Himself can take away the eternal punishment which I justly deserve.
4. Jesus did two important things as my substitute. First, He paid the penalty of death for me. Second, He obeyed God's law perfectly for me and gave me a title to eternal life. Jesus' work as substitute fits in perfectly with God's demands and the sinner's need.

Review Questions and Answers

1. *Who is the Savior of sinners?*

   The Savior is Jesus Christ who is truly God and truly man.
2. *What two great things did Jesus do to save sinners from sin and death?*

   1. Jesus paid the penalties which we sinners deserved. 2. Jesus gave to God the willing and perfect obedience which we owed God.
3. *How did Jesus pay the supreme penalty for sinners?*

   He paid for our sins by His accursed death on the cross of Calvary.
4. *Did Jesus save all sinners by His perfect work?*

   Jesus effectively saves those whom the Father has given Him before the foundation of the world.
5. *What are the three most common names of our Savior?*

   Jesus, Christ, and Lord are the three most common names of our Savior.

Digging Deeper

1. Which groups deny that Jesus was the Son of God?

2. Why do you consider the teaching of the Virgin Birth important?
3. What do such words as *reconciliation*, *satisfaction* and *sacrifice* mean in connection with the work of Jesus?
5. What do the *Canons of Dort* teach in the Second Head of Doctrine about the death of Jesus Christ?
6. Does the truth that Jesus substituted Himself only for a definite number of elect make God unfair?

LESSON 5

What I Confess

1. I believe that Jesus arose from the dead on the third day. This fact is precious in my life. Now I need never fear the power of death and the grave since I shall live forever with my living Lord.
2. I believe that Jesus of Nazareth is now ruling in heaven for the sake of the saved. He is my Teacher or Prophet who continues to lead me into the ways of truth. He is my High Priest who prays for me in the presence of God. He is my King who controls everything for the welfare of the saved and for the final glory of my God.
3. I believe that Jesus Christ is on His way back to our world. There are many signs which point to His return. I keep watching and waiting for His return. This return of Jesus is the climax of His glory and the climax of my salvation.
4. When Jesus returns, my body shall be raised from the dead to be joined with my soul. Then I shall appear before the judgment seat of Christ. Because Jesus is my Savior I do not fear Him as my Judge.
5. I am looking forward to the new universe which shall arise when Christ returns. In that new world God shall be perfectly praised and I shall be able to honor Him forever in glory. In the company of all the saved I shall adore my God forever.

Review Questions and Answers

1. *What is the resurrection of Christ?*
   Jesus came out of the grave because He had completely satisfied God's justice.

2. *Where did Jesus go forty days after His resurrection?*
   Jesus ascended into the presence of God to continue His work of saving our sinful world.

3. *What is the victorious Savior doing now?*
   He continues to work every day as our chief Prophet, only High Priest and eternal King.

4. *What has Christ promised for the future?*
   Christ will return to complete His work as Savior and Judge.

5. *What is the Christian's glorious hope?*
   The Christian hopes to live in the perfect presence of God in a new heaven and a new earth which Christ shall give at the end of time.

Digging Deeper

1. What threefold comfort does the resurrection of Jesus give the believer according to the *Heidelberg Catechism*, Question 45?
2. What does the *Heidelberg Cathechism*, Question 49, teach about the ascension of Jesus and the Christian life?
3. What is one of the reasons according to II Peter 3:9 why Jesus tarries in His return?
4. Which signs of Jesus' return are very much in evidence today?
5. What does Article XXXVII of the *Belgic Confession* teach about the last judgment?

LESSON 6

What I Confess

1. I praise the work of God the Holy Spirit in my life. It is the Holy Spirit who unites my life to Jesus Christ my Savior. Without this wonderful work of the Holy Spirit I would still be spiritually dead.
2. I believe that I am a born-again child of God. God the Holy Spirit came into my life and made a new creature out of me. I do not know just how the Holy Spirit did this but I do know that He did it all. Because God worked this miracle in my life I now am able and willing to confess Christ as my Savior and Lord.
3. I give God the glory for making me alive. I did not cooperate with the Holy Spirit in this work of regeneration. He opened the closed doors of my life and entered in. He softened my hard heart. Now I delight to do God's will and love God above all.
4. I believe that the Holy Spirit and Jesus Christ are working together in saving my life. Now that I am a regenerated person I know that Jesus Christ lives within my heart. My Savior's personal presence in my life is the biggest joy and strength of my life.
5. I believe that gospel preaching is very important. The Holy Spirit usually works in connection with this work of preaching to give dead sinners new life. I shall continue to pray that God may save others through the preaching of the gospel. I know in my own life that the gospel is the power of God unto salvation.
6. I have heard God's call to repentance in my own life. As my spiritual life grows I discover a deep sorrow for sins because I have wounded the love of God. The more I see of sin in my life and around my life the more I detest it and fight against it.

7. I believe in Jesus Christ as my Savior and Lord. I know something about His marvelous work and am convinced that it fits exactly the needs of my life. Not only do I know Jesus Christ but I trust Him completely. By God's grace I have abandoned my whole life to Him.
8. I know that I am justified by faith. God, my Holy Judge, no longer holds my sins against me. My sins are forgiven because of everything Jesus did for me. God declares the perfect work of Jesus to be mine, yes so completely that God now looks on me as if I did it myself. How I praise my Savior for His free and rich gift of salvation!
9. I realize that I am justified only in the way of faith. Nothing I do could possibly make me right with God. Even the best actions of my life are stained with sin. Even my faith does not save me. It is God, the Father, Son, and Holy Spirit, who saves me in the way of faith.
10. I know that I have been bought by the precious blood of Christ. I no longer belong to myself, but belong completely to my Savior. I shall try to glorify, praise, and serve my God completely. I realize this will demand much sacrifice, self-denial, and strength. But I can now do all things through Christ who strengthens me.

Review Questions and Answers

1. *Who is the Holy Spirit?*

   The Holy Spirit is the third person of the Trinity who applies Christ's work to our lives.

2. *What is the chief means which the Holy Spirit uses to apply Christ's work to our lives?*

   The Holy Spirit uses the preaching of the gospel which is true to the Scriptures.

3. *What is man's greatest need as an unsaved sinner?*

   Man needs to be made alive by the regenerating Spirit of God.

4. *What happens when a sinner receives this gift of regeneration?*

   The sinner becomes a new creature and begins to think, feel, and will differently than he did before he was made alive.

5. *What does it mean to repent of sin?*

   To repent means that a person admits his sin, sorrows on account of his sin, and breaks with sin.

6. *What does it mean to believe on the Lord Jesus Christ?*

   To believe means to know God's good news of salvation and to trust Him for personal forgiveness and eternal life because of the work of Jesus Christ.

7. *How do sinners get right with God?*

   Sinners believe that God the Judge declares them righteous because of the perfect work of Jesus Christ.

8. *Can a person's good deeds make him right with God?*
   A person's good deeds are not perfect and therefore they cannot help toward making him right with God.
9. *How does the saved sinner demonstrate that he is a genuine Christian?*
   The saved sinner tries to live a consecrated and God-honoring life in every way.

Digging Deeper

1. What were the signs accompanying the outpouring of the Holy Spirit? (Acts 2:1-6). What do these signs mean?
2. What do the *Canons of Dort*, Chapter III-IV, Articles 10-13 teach about regeneration? What does it mean that God never treats us as "stocks and blocks"? See *Canons of Dort*, Chapter III-IV, Article 16.
3. What do present-day Pentecostal sects teach about the spiritual gifts of the Holy Spirit? Why did the Holy Spirit use the gifts of "tongues" and "healing" in the early church?
4. What does the Reformed faith mean by the term *irresistible grace*?
5. What are the fruits of the Holy Spirit in the Christian life according to Galatians 5:22, 23?

LESSON 7

What I Confess

1. I believe that every Christian is made a member of the church of Jesus Christ by the Holy Spirit. This church is the one body of Jesus Christ, my Savior, in which every member has a place. Just as one finger is important to the proper health of my physical body so every church member is important for the spiritual health of the body of Jesus Christ.
2. I believe that it is possible to discover a genuine church of Jesus Christ in the face of the many denominations which one sees in every community. In trying to choose the best church I look for the three marks of the true church. These three marks are: 1. preaching which is true to the whole Bible; 2. proper use of the sacraments of Holy Baptism and the Lord's Supper; 3. the loyal exercise of Christian discipline.
3. I believe that Christ Jesus established three special offices or tasks in the church. These offices are the ministry, the eldership, and the deaconate. Each of these officebearers is reflecting the work

of Jesus Christ in the church in a special way. I shall honor and respect these workmen as they work on behalf of my Savior.

4. The organizational setup of the church is important so that all things may be done decently and in order within the church. Since I am a living member of the whole I shall pray and work within the framework of this organization. I shall support the whole church with my whole life so that I may show my grateful love to Jesus Christ.
5. I believe that Jesus Christ is the Head and King of the church. I shall work and pray that I, together with the whole membership and the officers, may faithfully and obediently serve Christ our common Savior and Lord. I promise to do my part in building up the body of Christ.
6. Christ Jesus must feed the new life which He gave me. I am as dependent upon Him for this nourishment as I was for the gift of spiritual life itself. I am grateful that He provides the means of grace and I promise to use them faithfully.
7. The Word of God is the chief means of grace in my life. I shall faithfully attend the preaching of the gospel in public worship. But I also realize the need for daily fellowship with my God through His Word. In my personal devotions as well as in family devotions I shall continue to work and pray that Christ may feed my life with His Word.
8. As a believer I am grateful for the sacrament of Holy Baptism. Even though I may have been baptized many years ago the meaning of my baptism continues to be a blessing for my life. Baptism is a sign and seal of my union with God and of the cleansing I receive in the blood of Jesus Christ.
9. The Lord's Supper is another sacrament which Christ has established to strengthen my spiritual life. At the table of the Lord I believe I am fed with the crucified body and shed blood of my Savior. It is a joy to proclaim the Lord's death until He comes.
10. A healthy Christian is a praying Christian. In my prayers I shall adore my God, confess my sins, give thanksgiving, and present my petition. All this I must do in the name of Jesus, my Savior.

Review Questions and Answers

1. *What is the Church of Jesus Christ?*

   The Church is a band of believing sinners who rely on their Savior for salvation.

2. *How can a person discover a true church of Christ?*

   There are three main characteristics of a true church: 1. The preaching of the gospel must be loyal to the whole Bible. 2. The sacraments of Holy Baptism and the Holy Supper must be administered according to the regulations of God's Word. 3. Christian supervision must be carried on loyally and lovingly.

3. *What three offices are found in the Church?*
   The office of minister, elder, and deacon are found in the Church.

4. *Why must the Christian faithfully attend church services?*
   Christ Jesus uses the preaching of the Word and the administration of the sacraments to strengthen the faith of Christian people.

5. *What is the sacrament of Holy Baptism?*
   It is a sign and a seal that our sins are washed away by the blood and Spirit of Jesus Christ.

6. *What is the sacrament of Holy Communion?*
   It is a sign and a seal that Christians are fed by the true body and blood of Christ through a mysterious working of the Holy Spirit.

7. *What is the deep meaning of prayer?*
   Prayer is that holy and precious fellowship in which man draws close to God and God comes nigh to man.

8. *What is the Lord's Prayer?*
   It is the perfect prayer which Jesus taught His disciples, the elements of which we ought to practice in our prayers.

Digging Deeper

1. What kind of sorrow did Esau experience after he sold his birthright to Jacob? See Hebrews 12:16, 17.
2. In what four ways can a person receive the Word of the gospel according to the Parable of the Sower in Matthew 13?
3. What does James 2:17-26 teach about faith and good works?
4. How does Article XXIII of the *Belgic Confession* describe the blessing of justification?
5. What is the doctrine of the perseverance of the saints according to the *Canons of Dort*, Chapter V?
6. What is the ecumenical movement?
7. What does Article XXVIII of the *Belgic Confession* teach about joining a true church?
8. What are the marks of a false church according to Article XXIX of the *Belgic Confession*?
9. What are some of the ways in which you can take an active part in your church?
10. Why is membership in secret, oath-bound religious societies which teach false doctrine inconsistent with membership in a Christian church?

11. How can you carry on personal and family devotions?
12. Is it absolutely necessary for salvation to be baptized? What does the Roman Catholic Church teach about the necessity of baptism?
13. What does the *Heidelberg Catechism*, Answer 80, say about the Roman Catholic Sacrament of the mass?
14. Why do some denominations urge their members to establish Christian day schools? How is Christian education related to infant baptism?
15. If God determines whatsoever comes to pass, why must the Christian pray?

LESSON 8

What I Confess

1. Since it pleases God to rule my life through the authority of parents and others, I shall honor, respect, and obey these authorities for God's sake. As a parent I shall try to train my children in the fear and knowledge of the Lord.
2. I shall try to love my neighbor as myself. This includes seeking the best for him in every possible way. I shall respect his life, his home, his property, and his name. In a life of positive love toward my neighbor I shall continue to glorify and honor my God.
3. I believe that God's law penetrates deep into my heart. God's will must mold and fashion my desires. Thus I shall listen to the words of my Savior who commands me to seek first the kingdom of God and His righteousness. As I do this God shall provide me with all that is necessary for this life and the life to come.
4. The more I seek to honor God by obeying His law the more I realize the extent of my sinfulness. From God's law I learn to see myself as I really am in the sight of God. Seeing this I take refuge in Jesus Christ as my personal Savior.
5. As a thankful Christian I shall try to live according to all the commandments of my God. His law shall be the standard by which I measure all my conduct. His law has become the delight and joy of my life. I will keep it ever before me as my guide for a God-glorifying life.
6. I believe I owe God new obedience. This means that I try to obey God's law in order to show how thankful I am for being saved by God's grace. My new obedience is not a condition for salvation but rather a fruit of my salvation. I have learned to delight in the law of my Lord.

7. I owe my supreme loyalty and deepest love to the one God, Father, Son, and Holy Spirit. He is my chief joy and supreme delight. I shall fight against the sin of setting up other gods in my life.
8. I know that I can worship God only in and through Jesus Christ. I shall study God's Word diligently to discover the proper ways of bringing my worship unto Him. I shall worship neither graven nor mental images of my God.
9. God's name is very precious to me. God's name is the way in which He makes Himself known to me and comes into my life. I shall properly reverence and honor His name and war against the sin of profanity.
10. The Lord's Day is a delight in my life. It is a day of spiritual refreshment, physical rest, and special Christian service. In these times when many fail to keep the Lord's Day holy, I shall use it for the purposes which God intended.

Review Questions and Answers

1. *What is the obedience which the Christian owes to God?*
   It is a new obedience which arises from a grateful personality made alive by the Holy Spirit.
2. *Why does the Christian try to live in harmony with God's law?*
   The Christian obeys because he has been saved and not in order to become saved.
3. *How many commandments are found in the first part of the law?*
   Four commandments are found which deal with God's honor and glory directly.
4. *What does Christ teach as a summary of the first table of the law?*
   Thou shalt love the Lord thy God with all thy heart, with all thy soul, with all thy mind and with all thy strength.
5. *How many commandments are found in the second table of the law?*
   The second table of the law contains five commandments which deal with our duties to God and our neighbor. The fifth commandment forms a bridge between the first and second tables of God's law.
6. *What summary did Jesus give of the second table of the law?*
   Thou shalt love thy neighbor as thyself.
7. *Can the Christian obey God's law perfectly?*
   This is impossible as long as we live on this earth, but he does earnestly try to please God in every way.

8. *Why must we pay attention to God's law?*
By listening carefully to God's law we learn to know our sins better and we also have a rule to guide us in living a consecrated and God-glorifying life.

Digging Deeper

1. Why must the Christian perform good works, according to the *Heidelberg Catechism*, Answer 86?
2. What does Isaiah 64:6 teach about the nature of the Christian's good works?
3. In what ways can "the community spirit" and "democracy" be false gods?
4. How would you answer a Seventh-Day Adventist's view of the Sabbath day?
5. What is a "reward of merit" and a "reward of grace"? See *Belgic Confession*, Article XXIV.
6. In what way are Christians not under the law, and in what sense are they under the law? Why is the law read in some churches every Sunday?
7. What is the Christian's duty toward human government according to Romans 13:1-7?
8. Is capital punishment right or wrong?
9. What are some of the principles the Bible sets forth for Christian giving? See Matthew 10:8; II Corinthians 9:7; Romans 12:8; I Corinthians 16:2.
10. What does your church teach about divorce?
11. How is Christian liberty related to God's law?
12. What does the Bible teach about abortion?

A Basic Christian Vocabulary

A

Adiaphora. Matters of conduct which are neither sinful or righteous in themselves but which may become legitimate or illegitimate in the Christian life according to circumstances.

Adoption. The act of God's love whereby He takes saved sinners into His family and bestows all the rights of sonship upon them as children of God.

Adoration. The act of reverently reflecting upon God's many perfections and giving loving praise to Him for His own sake.

Annihilationism. A false teaching that the unsaved wicked will not suffer eternal punishment in hell but will finally cease to be as if they had never lived.

Anti-Christ. One who is against Christ. Just before Christ returns there will probably arise one individual who will concentrate in his life all imaginable evil against Christ.

Apocrypha. Those religious books which are not included in the Holy Bible because they were not inspired by God the Holy Spirit.

Apostasy. A falling away from the truth of God as revealed in the Bible, in words and deeds by one person, a church, or a nation.

Arminianism. A system of doctrine which regards God's actions as somewhat limited by and dependent upon the free actions of man. This system derives its name from a Dutch theologian named Jacobus Arminius.

Assurance. The conviction that a person is presently saved by grace and will surely enter into heaven, which a believer may attain as he rightly uses the means of grace and knows the witness of the Holy Spirit in his heart.

Atonement. The satisfaction of God's justice made by Jesus Christ, which was necessary for the forgiveness of sinners.

Calvinism. The system of truth which acknowledges the absolute sovereignty of God and man's total dependence on God for every part of his life, faith, and salvation. It is consistent Biblical Christianity which received its basic expression in the writings of the Genevan Reformer, John Calvin.

Canon of Scripture. The list of the books of the Bible which are recognized as inspired by God the Holy Spirit.

Catholic Church. The universal world-wide church of God as distinguished from any special congregation or denomination. When the word *Roman* is used it refers to a special organization of churches under the control of a Pope who lives in Vatican City at Rome.

Congregation. A group of Christ-confessing sinners of like faith gathered in one place for the purpose of worship.

Conscience. The function of a human being which registers approval when a person's actions fit in with his standards of conduct and disapproval when his actions violate his standards of what is right and wrong.

Conversion. The sinner's turning from sin to God,which is the effect of regeneration and which includes repentance and faith.

Covenant of Grace. That gracious arrangement of God made with believers and their children in which God promises eternal salvation in the way of repentance and faith.

Covenant of Works. That arrangement of God with Adam, the first man, in which God promised full fellowship with man and his seed on the condition of perfect and personal obedience.

Creation. The act of God's will by which He made all things good for the praise and glory of His name.

D

Deity of Christ. The truth that Jesus of Nazareth was and is the only true God, one in whom dwelleth all the fullness of the Godhead bodily.

Depravity, Total. The truth that the unsaved sinner is corrupted by sin in every part of his personality and completely unable and unwilling to do any good which is pleasing to God.

Divine Decrees. God's eternal purpose in which He has foreordained whatsoever comes to pass. All of God's decrees form the counsel of His will.

E

Election. God's unconditional and sovereign choice of certain men in Christ unto final salvation.

Eschatology. The Biblical teaching concerning the last things. These teachings include such matters as the state of man after death, the return of Christ, the signs announcing His second coming, the resurrection, the judgment, and eternal life.

Eternity of God. The perfection of God by which He lives independent of all the limitations of time and succession of moments.

Exaltation of Christ. The life of Jesus Christ which He now lives as having been rewarded by God for His perfect work. It consists of His resurrection from the dead, His ascension into heaven, His sitting at the right hand of God, and His return at the end of time.

Excommunication. The final step in Christian discipline in which the unrepentant church member is solemnly excluded from the fellowship of the church until such a time as he turns from his sins.

F

Faith, Historical. A mere agreement with the truths of the Bible as a matter of historical fact without personal trust in God and Jesus Christ for salvation.

Faith, Temporary. A faith which resembles true faith but which does not proceed from a new-born life and which withers and disappears under the pressures of sin and persecution.

Faith, True. "A sure knowledge, whereby I hold for truth all that God has revealed to us in His Word, and also a firm confidence which the Holy Spirit works in my heart by the gospel, that not only to others, but to me also, remission of sins, everlasting righteousness and salvation are freely given by God, merely of grace, only for the sake of Christ's merit" (*Heidelberg Catechism*, Answer 21)

Fall of Man. The act which took place when Adam and Eve ate of the forbidden fruit in the garden of Eden and which plunged mankind from the situation of perfection and joy into sin and misery.

Five Points of Calvinism. Five interrelated Biblical truths explained in the *Canons of Dort*, one of the doctrinal standards of the Christian Reformed Church. These five truths are: 1. unconditional election; 2. limited or definite atonement; 3. total depravity; 4. irresistible grace; 5. perseverance of the saints. These five truths form an answer to five errors held by Arminians.

Foreordination. God's determination from all eternity of everything that takes place in time.

Forgiveness of Sins. The act of God by which the sinner's guilt is no longer charged to him and he is thus released from paying the penalty of sins. It is also called *Pardon*.

G

Glorification. The final stage of salvation of God's elect at which time they are taken to heaven in the moment of death and receive a new body and a new universe when Christ comes again.

Good Works. Those acts of man which proceed from a true faith, according to the law of God and which are dedicated to God's glory.

Gospel. The good news of salvation which God provides for sinners in the work of Jesus Christ.

Grace of God. The goodness and favor of God which God gives to those people who are not entitled to it and who deserve His wrath and punishment because of sin.

Grace, Common. A special kind of grace or favor which God gives to all sinners without distinction and which includes many blessings for this life but does not include salvation.

Grace, Special. That free favor which God gives only to the elect and which brings about their salvation.

H

Heaven. This refers to: 1. the celestial world (Genesis 1:1); 2. that place where God's presence and glory are concentrated; 3. the future home of the saved (II Cor. 5:1).

Hell. The place of eternal punishment prepared particularly for Satan and his angels where all unsaved sinners will be banished from the blessed presence of God.

Heresy. An unbiblical doctrine which is contrary to the accepted creeds or doctrinal standards of a church, which, if left unchallenged, would eventually destroy the witness of the church to God's truth.

Heretic. A person who holds to and propagates a heresy.

Holiness of God. God's awful majesty and His infinite and absolute separation from all that is sinful.

Hope. The believer's eager expectation of final glory and joy in a re-created universe which shall be given to him when Christ returns.

Humiliation of Christ. The position which Christ took under the law of God at the time of His birth. While in this position He experienced the wrath of God, the miseries of life, and final banishment from this life in His death and burial. This position ended for Jesus at the time of His resurrection from the dead.

I

Incarnation. The act of God the Son in taking to Himself a complete human nature, body and soul, to win salvation for sinners.

Independence of God. That perfection by which God is perfectly sufficient to Himself and in no way whatever dependent on anyone or anything.

Infallibility of Scripture. The Biblical teaching that the Bible is absolutely trustworthy and free from all errors.

Infinity of God. That perfection of God by which He is completely boundless, without any limits as to space and time.

Immanence of God. That perfection of God by which He is everywhere present in the created world. It is also called the omnipresence of God.

Imputation. The act of a judge by which something is reckoned over unto one's account or laid to the charge or credit of someone. What is reckoned or charged forms the basis for a declaration by the judge either until acquittal or condemnation. The Bible speaks of three major imputations: 1. of Adam's sin to the whole human race; 2. of the elect's sin to Jesus Christ; 3. of Christ's righteousness to the believing sinner.

Iniquity. A word for sin which includes the ideas of perverseness, the absence of justice, and wickedness.

Inspiration of the Bible. The act of God, the Holy Spirit, by which He influenced the writers of the Bible books to write the exact words and thoughts which God intended them to write.

Intercession of Christ. The work of the exalted Savior in heaven whereby He pleads the cause of each and every true child of God.

J

Justification. An act of God, the Judge, in which He graciously forgives sins and declares us perfectly innocent in His righteousness. This declaration is based on the perfect righteousness of Christ which is reckoned or imputed to the believer's life. This blessing can only be received in the way of faith.

K

Keys of the Kingdom. The authority of church government and discipline which Christ, the head and King of the church, has given to the lawfully elected officers of His church.

Kingdom of God. The rulership of God established in and acknowledged by the hearts of the regenerated sinner which is partly realized in this age but which shall reach its full realization when Christ comes a second time.

L

Legalism. The wrong theory that one can become right with God by obeying the law of God. This error is seen clearly in the lives of the Pharisees who thought their obedience was acceptable to God.

Liberty, Christian. The freedom of the saved sinner from the wrath of God, the guilt of sin, the curse of the law, and the power of sin.

Longsuffering of God. That perfection of God by which He patiently bears with the evil in spite of their long-continued disobedience.

Love of God. That perfection of God which moves Him to give Himself in fellowship to sinners in Jesus Christ.

M

Means of Grace. The ordinary means which Christ Jesus uses to bring the blessings of salvation into sinner's lives. Christ uses especially the Word, the sacraments, and prayer to apply effectively His work in the lives of the elect.

Mediator. One who stands between two parties who are at odds. Jesus Christ is the only mediator between the offended God and the offending sinner.

Mercy of God. That perfection of God by which He acts to take pity on the miserable sinner and relieve His distress.

Merit. That which is earned. Merit is in contrast with grace which cannot be earned by man's work. Christ merited salvation and graciously gives salvation to whom He will.

Messiah. A Hebrew word meaning "anointed." An anointed person was set apart to perform a certain work. Christ is the Greek term meaning the same thing. Jesus Christ was anointed to be the perfect prophet, priest, and king.

Millennium. The thousand year period spoken of in Revelation 20:1-10. During this period Christ reigns and Satan is kept in check. We believe this thousand year period to refer to the time between Christ's ascension into heaven and His final return at the end of time.

Miracle. A special event in the physical world caused by the direct activity of God which points beyond itself to the saving work of God in Jesus Christ through the Holy Spirit.

N

Natures of Christ. Refers to the mystery of Jesus who is both perfectly human and perfectly divine.

O

Obedience of Christ. The work of Jesus Christ in which He took care of the guilt of sin and met the penal requirements of God's law. This is often called Christ's *passive* obedience. Christ also perfectly fulfilled the demands of God's law. This is often called Christ's *active* obedience. This two-fold obedience is the ground for forgiveness of sins.

Original Guilt. The liability of punishment which was Adam's because of his first sin and which is reckoned or imputed by God to all members of the human race.

Original Sin. The first sin of Adam which became the root out of which all the sin and misery of the world has come.

P

Perfectionism. The teaching that it is possible for a Christian, in this life, to reach a position where he no longer commits any sin.

Perseverance of the Saints. The Biblical teaching that the regenerated sinner can neither totally or finally fall away from salvation but shall be preserved by the abiding grace of God.

Predestination. God's eternal determination of the final end of every individual among angels and men.

Probationary Command. The commandment which God gave to Adam and Eve in Paradise, not to eat of the tree of the knowledge of good and evil, in which God tested our first parents with respect to their obedience to God.

Propitiation. The removing of God's displeasure and wrath by Jesus Christ as He fully satisfied the justice and holiness of God. Christ is the propitiation for our sins.

Providence. The everywhere-present activity of God whereby He preserves the whole order of creation and governs all things and events unto their appointed end.

R

Reconciliation. The root idea is to change thoroughly from one position to another. By virtue of Christ's perfect work the elect are removed from a position of estrangement and alienation into a position of friendship and companionship with God.

Redemption. God's work of meeting all the requirements for the salvation of sinners by which God freed the elect sinner from the bondage of sin.

Regeneration. The act of God the Holy Spirit by which He makes the spiritually dead sinner alive. It is also called the *New Birth*.

Reprobation. God's sovereign act of passing by certain sinners not chosen to salvation and His righteous condemnation of such sinners to endure the just rewards of their sins.

Revelation. God's activity by which He makes truth known to men.

Revelation, General. God's action of communicating truth to man through the created world of nature, the history of man, and man's own conscience.

Revelation, Special. God's action of communicating truth to some men in and through the Scriptures.

Righteousness of God. That perfection of God by which He as the Holy One acts in perfect harmony with His law. It is also called the *Justice* of God by which He rewards good and punishes evil.

S

Sacrament. A holy religious ceremony instituted by Christ in which the grace of God in Christ and the blessings of the covenant of grace are pictured, sealed, and applied to believers who respond in faith and loyalty to God. The New Testament church observes the sacraments of Baptism and the Lord's Supper.

Sanctification. The work of God whereby the saved sinner is refashioned in the whole man after the ways of God so that he dies more and more to sin and lives unto righteousness.

Satisfaction of Christ. Christ's act of sacrificing Himself in order to meet the demands of God's justice in the place of each one of the elect. It is also called the *Vicarious Atonement* and *Substitutionary Atonement*.

Sovereignty of God. That perfection of God's absolute authority over His created universe by which He does everything for His own glory according to the counsel of His will.

T

Temptation. The enticement of a person by Satan, the sinful world, or the sinful nature of man to commit sin by offering some seeming advantage to the person being tempted.

Transgression. A word meaning sin which describes the act as a stepping over the line laid down in God's law.

Trinity. The Biblical teaching that one God exists in three separate persons—the Father, the Son, and the Holy Spirit, who are the same in substance and equal in glory.

Truth. That which is in harmony with God's nature and revelation.

V

Vow. A solemn promise made to God. Sometimes called an oath which is a religious activity in which the person swearing solemnly calls God to witness what he promises or asserts.

W

Wrath of God. God's perfectly-righteous anger at sin and His act of inflicting deserved punishments upon guilty sinners.

Z

Zeal. A passionate enthusiasm or fervent desire to maintain a person or cause. The motives of the zealous person together with the object of his zeal determine whether it is sinful or righteous zeal.